An End to Innocence

AN END
TO INNOCENCE

FACING LIFE WITHOUT ILLUSIONS

Sheldon Kopp

MACMILLAN PUBLISHING CO., INC.
New York

Macmillan Publishing Co., Inc.
866 Third Avenue, New York, N.Y. 10022
Collier Macmillan Canada, Ltd.

Library of Congress Cataloging in Publication Data
Kopp, Sheldon B   1929–
An end to innocence.
Includes bibliographical references.
1. Innocence (Psychology)   2. Psychotherapy
patients—Cases, clinical reports, statistics.
3. Kopp, Sheldon B., 1929–   4. Psychologists—
United States—Biography.   I. Title.
BF575.I48K66   616.8'914   78–12450
ISBN 0–02–566470–0

First Printing 1978

Printed in the United States of America

Contents

Acknowledgments

Grateful acknowledgment is made to:

Spring Publications, Zurich/New York/Dallas, for permission to quote from "The Three Feathers" by the Brothers Grimm as quoted in *An Introduction to the Interpretation of Fairy Tales* by Marie-Louise von Franz, 1970.

Columbia University Press, New York, for permission to quote from *The Insects* by Url Lanham, 1964.

EdITS Publishers, San Diego, California, for permission to quote from *The Naked Therapist* by Sheldon B. Kopp, 1976.

The *Journal of Contemporary Psychotherapy* for permission to quote from "Person Envy" by Sheldon B. Kopp (Volume 6, No. 2, Summer 1974).

Science and Behavior Books, Palo Alto, California, for permission to quote from *Guru* by Sheldon B. Kopp, 1971; *If You Meet the Buddha on the Road, Kill Him!* by Sheldon B. Kopp, 1972; *The Hanged Man* by Sheldon B. Kopp, 1975; and *This Side of Tragedy* by Sheldon B. Kopp, 1977.

The Viking Press, New York, and William Heineman Ltd., London, for permission to quote from *Of Mice and Men* by John Steinbeck. Copyright 1937, renewed © 1965 by John Steinbeck.

PART ONE

NOSTALGIA AND REVENGE

. . . nostalgia is a form of revenge, and revenge a form of nostalgia.

Maria Isabel Barreno,
Maria Teresa Horta,
Maria Velko de Costa,
The Three Marias: Portuguese Letters

1

Once Upon a Time

Life can be counted on to provide all the pain that any of us might possibly need. At times, each of us adds a measure of needless suffering to that already weighty inevitable burden. We insist that life's random mishaps and calamities should not be happening to us. By dramatizing our plight with an anguished sense of personal injustice we exaggerate the pain of chance mishaps.

Denying that these *are* the good old days, we remain nostalgically attached to an earlier time and place that we can *almost* remember as having been better. Petulantly longing for a future that will make everything right once more, we miss making what we can of this mixed bag of world-as-it-is-now. Desperately holding onto the fairy-tale vision of a life in which the face of the enemy is clear and the good guys always win, we waste our lives in waiting for the happy ending.

If we are not to miss out on those random moments of happiness that adults may have, we must learn to give up the deceptively comforting illusions of childhood. We can be free to live our lives as we choose only if we are willing to risk facing the often unforsee-able consequences of our acts, knowing that there is no one else to take care of us. Partial freedom and limited happiness are all that are available. But to receive the rewards of even those less-than-perfect bounties, grown-ups must pay the price of the loss of inno-cence.

As very small children, most of us saw our world as a safe, familiar well-ordered place. Too soon, we began to find it filled with danger, contradiction, and unfairness. Eventually, just "being good" no longer provided assurance that someone would take care of us. Too often, as adolescents, we found ourselves disappointed and betrayed.

Finally grown up, we find that everything has changed. Lost and alone, uprooted and unloved, at times we all long for home. This painful longing is soulfully expressed in the poignant lines of a lovely old spiritual sung by slaves torn from the world they once knew:

> Sometimes I feel like a motherless child,
> Sometimes I feel like a motherless child,
> Sometimes I feel like a motherless child,
> A long way from home,
> A long, long way from home.[1]

Each of us has experienced that yearning to return to a time and place in which we felt so loved and well taken care of that it was safe to be completely trusting. Even those who never had such a haven may yearn for it.

Growing up often means facing the anguished isolation of no longer belonging as we wander in exile through a strange world that makes no sense. Each of us must make his or her own separate way through an indifferent, unfamiliar landscape in which good is not necessarily rewarded, nor evil punished. Adding to the confusion, at times we find ourselves or others graced with unearned love and happiness or burdened with "undeserved" calamity and pain.

For some of us, it seems as though this is the way it has always been. So little protected and so badly hurt even as children, we dare not trust again. Self-protective distrust results in our missing whatever loving closeness we might have with other grown-ups.

Others of us blame ourselves for having lost our parents' acceptance. Burdened by feelings of guilt, we waste our adult lives in endless attempts to be good. If we can only be *really* good, surely then someone will take care of us. Clinging to outgrown innocence, we are needlessly disappointed again and again as we miss what we might get out of taking care of ourselves.

What's a grown-up to do?

The futile search for the lost security and trust of the nursing infant means missing out on rewards of adult independence. The illusion of reclaiming such innocence requires the dangerous immersion in fanatic devotion to a cause or system that promises to make everything right again.

The Flower Children of the sixties started out trying to love and trust everyone. They ended up overdosed, busted, disillusioned. The Administration said, "Trust us." In return, they gave us Vietnam, the FBI, the CIA, and Watergate. The alternative of paranoid distrust can protect us from ever being hurt again, but the cost of such safety is even greater loneliness.

God is dead, and no one else seems to care. How are we to love in the absence of illusions? What sense does it make to live openly and decently? How are we to know when, how, and whom to trust? Is being paranoid a way of going crazy, or a way of going sane?

Once upon a time, when we were very small children, there were people we could trust. Otherwise we would not have survived. The physical needs of a helpless and dependent child must be met by caring adults, or the child will die. But parenting requires more than this. Protection and nurturance for the child's psychological vulnerability must also be available.

One of the ways that grown-ups take care of children is by telling them fairy tales. These truncated myths are poetically symbolic ways of instructing and comforting a child. Fairy tales instruct by teaching the idealized virtues that each culture purports to value and those behaviors that each deems "appropriate." Promising the rewards of a well-ordered universe, these simple tales assure the child that being "good" will always lead to fulfillment of our heart's desires.

Fairy tales do not teach what living in the adult world is all about. Purified and simplified for the ears of innocent children, they describe the world as the culture insists it *should* be.

All children start out helpless and dependent. Their innocence needs to be preserved until they are competent and independent enough to make their own way. For a while, it is helpful to protect them from the ambiguity of the inevitably unmanageable experiences of a life that so often turns out to be both unpredictable and unfair. Later there will be time to attempt a "reconciliation of consciousness with . . . the monstrous nature of this terrible game that is life." [2]

The pretend atmosphere of fairy tales shelters the child from the overwhelming uncertainties and the confusing sense of helplessness that adults must face from time to time. No matter how scary or violent a fairy tale, the struggle between good and evil is always clear. Good always triumphs. In this simple, unshaded opposition between black and white, the poverty of subtle content is balanced by the clarity and incisiveness of the moral forces. The characters are prepackaged, unchanging figures, pure forms in external classic struggle.

Within the hero himself we find no psychological conflicts, he is not partly this and partly that—each quality is personified in the simplest form: courage is opposed to cowardice, envy to innocence, kindness to malice, renunciation and self-sacrifice to unrestrained lust or greed.[3]

As a simple example of a typical fairy tale, consider "The Three Feathers" by the Brothers Grimm:

There was once a king who had three sons. Two were intelligent but the third did not talk much and was stupid and was called Dummling. The king was old and weak and thought about his death and did not know which of his sons should inherit the kingdom. So he told them to go out into the world and the one who brought him the most beautiful carpet would be king when he died. To prevent any quarrelling he went outside the castle, blew three feathers into the air and said: "As they fly, so you must go." One feather went towards the east, the other to the west, and the third just a little way straight ahead, where it fell to the ground. So one brother went to the right, the other to the left, and they laughed at Dummling who had to stay where the third feather had fallen.

Dummling sat down and was very sad, but then suddenly he noticed that there was a trapdoor beside the feather. He lifted it up, found steps descending and went down into the earth. There he came to another door at which he knocked. . . . The door opened and Dummling saw an enormous fat toad sitting there surrounded by a circle of little toads. The fat toad asked him what he wanted and he answered that he would like to have the finest and most beautiful carpet. The toad called a young toad saying: . . . "Bring me the big box." The young toad fetched the big box, which the big toad opened, and from it she gave Dummling a beautiful carpet, a carpet so beautiful and so delicate that it could never have been woven on earth. He thanked her for it and climbed up again.

The other two brothers thought their youngest brother too silly ever to be able to find anything so they bought some coarse linen stuff which the first shepherd-woman they met was wearing around her body and took it home to the king. At the same time Dummling came home with his beautiful carpet and when the king saw it he said: "By rights the kingdom should go to the youngest." But the other two gave their father no peace, saying that it was impossible to give Dummling the kingdom because he was so stupid and they asked for another competition.

So the king said that the one who could bring the most beautiful ring should have the kingdom. Again he performed the same ritual with the three feathers. Again the two eldest went to the east and to the west and for Dummling the feather went straight ahead and fell down by the door in the ground. Again he went down to the fat toad and told her that he wanted the most beautiful ring. She again had the big box fetched and from it gave him a ring which gleamed with precious stones and was so beautiful that no goldsmith on earth could have made it. The other two again laughed about Dummling who wanted to hunt for a gold ring the king again said that the kingdom belonged to him. But the cartwheel and brought that to the king. When Dummling showed his gold ring the king again said the the kingdom belonged to him. But the two elder brothers tormented the king until he set a third competition and said that the one who brought home the most beautiful wife should have the kingdom. He blew the three feathers again and they fell as before.

Dummling went to the fat toad and said that he had to take home the most beautiful woman. "Oh," said the toad, "the most beautiful woman is not just handy, but you shall have her." She gave him a hollowed-out carrot to which six mice were harnessed, and Dummling said sadly: "What shall I do with that?" The toad answered that he should take one of her little toads and put it into the carriage. He took one at random out of the circle and put it in the yellow carriage. She had scarcely sat in it before she was transformed into a beautiful girl, the carrot into a coach, and the six mice into six horses. He kissed the girl and drove away with the horses and brought her to the king. His brothers, who had not taken any trouble to look for a beautiful woman, came back with the first two peasant women they met. When the king saw them he said: "The kingdom goes to the youngest after my death." But the two brothers again deafened the king with their cries, saying that they couldn't permit that, and requested that the one whose wife could jump through a ring which hung in the middle of the room should have the preference. They thought that the peasant women would be able to do that because they would be strong but that the delicate girl would jump to her death. The old king agreed and the two peasant women jumped through the ring, but they were so awkward that they fell and broke their thick arms and legs. Thereupon the beautiful girl whom Dummling had brought sprang as lightly as a deer through the ring. So no further objection was possible. Dummling got the crown and ruled in wisdom for a long time.[4]

Like Cinderella, Beauty (of "Beauty and the Beast"), and the central characters of many other fairy tales, Dummling is the youngest, the humblest, the most obedient, and the most sincere of the children. Despite the envious conniving of more worldly, less worthy siblings, for his innocence Dummling alone is rewarded.

There are other more complex psychological interpretations of fairy tales. The child's listening to didactic cautionary tales is considered therapeutically helpful in learning to adjust to adult "realities." But the psychoanalytic vision of "reality" is as arbitrary an illusion as any other. Imbuing life with a manageable order, it encourages hope for more meaning and certainty than experience ever confirms. One prolific contemporary Freudian, Bruno Bettelheim, applauds the message he believes that fairy tales get across to the child:

... that a struggle against severe difficulties in life is unavoidable, is an intrinsic part of human existence. ...

So far so good. Unfortunately he goes on to complete the message in terms of the adult fairy-tale ethos of residual psychoanalytic innocence, saying:

but if one does not shy away, but steadfastly meets unexpected and often unjust hardships, *one masters all obstacles and at the end emerges victorious.*[5]

In this book, I have chosen to limit my own discussion of fairy tales to the ways in which they are used to maintain and to nurture the innocence of the young. When I write of the innocence of children I refer to that guileless trust out of which comes spontaneous action without evil intention. I do not mean that the expression of such innocence is restricted to joyful, loving behavior that cannot harm anyone else. It certainly is not. But for the innocent child, even the frustrated venting of anger is offered as a spontaneous way of reestablishing the natural order of life. It is an authentic response to immediate pain. When the pain is gone, so is the destructiveness.

There is no harm in maintaining a child's need to believe in a world that can be trusted, at least for a while. Gradually, as he or she grows, there will be time enough to learn about life's unfairness. But, if the experience is not to be brutally overwhelming, this coming of age must be paced to the child's growing strength.

My own children enjoyed believing in Santa Claus for a time. By the age of six or seven, each had heard from older children that "there ain't no Santa Claus." It was a time to ask my wife and myself, "Is Santa Claus real or pretend?"

We would answer the questions by saying, "The story of Santa Claus is fun for all of us. Whether Santa is real or pretend, you will have your Christmas and *we* will leave presents for you under the tree. When each of you is old enough, you must decide for yourself whether the story of Santa Claus is true or just made up to make children happy."

Having reached that particular stage of demythologizing, during the days preceding his last innocent Christmas each of my sons went ahead and wrote his letter to Santa Claus, "just in case." At the same time, each protested: "I really know that it's the mothers and fathers who leave the presents under the tree, but you never can tell for sure."

We allowed each one to let go of this piece of innocence at his own pace. A couple of Christmases later, each one joined us in doing the same for his younger brother.

As they grew older, we made sure to let them know that *we* gave them Christmas presents just because we loved them, not because they were good or bad. Soon each of them made or bought Christmas presents to leave under the tree for the other members of the family. Each learned to do this out of a spirit of giving and because the rest of us were important to him. I am grateful to our culture for providing the contemporary fairy tale of Santa Claus as a way of helping my kids to learn to be generous, and as an opportunity for me to see each through one piece of his needed loss of innocence.

The family can offer the easing support needed during that painful transition that marks the child's loss of innocence in coming of age. Imperfect as any loving family may be, it can at best provide an atmosphere filled with general goodwill, honesty, and individual consideration. Within this atmosphere each child needs to know that he or she has a special place. This sense of security serves as a temporary hedge against the impersonal arbitrariness that will have to be faced someday in the grown-up world. It can go a long way toward providing the needed feeling that some people can be trusted and that the child knows himself (or herself) to be one of those people. Children can start to learn how to encompass future disillusionments as they begin to encounter bits of arbitrariness even within their own loving families.

The telling of reassuring fairy tales need not be restricted to situations in which the child sits on the parent's lap to be told a traditional story that begins "Once upon a time . . ." and ends with ". . . And so they lived happily ever after." Each home has its own myths and idealizations of what the family and the outside world are all about. A child may be told, "In our family, we always keep our promises," or "We Italians (or Jews, or Irish, or whatever) always stick together," or "If you work hard and always try to do your very best, people will respect you."

Beliefs such as these are reassuring to young children. But such conceptions must not be too far from the truth. That way, no great harm will be done when eventually they are discredited by the child's later experiences.

An older child may learn that what was first believed does not *always* turn out to be true. Still *sometimes* things work out in a way that partially validates these early expectations. In growing up, such a child can retain a realistic measure of hope and trust. Modified by outside-the-family experiences of adolescence and early adulthood, the original innocent attitude can be developed into a more complex world-view without the person being stuck with a sense of having been tricked and misled.

For some children, the protective-family fairy tales are utterly destroyed by outside forces. One night a fire breaks out and the next day a family finds itself suddenly homeless. A series of unexpected fatal accidents and terminal illnesses decimate another family.

There have been times when political uprootings have separated and devastated whole communities of families. Imagine the shattered innocence of children whose families fell victim to the enslavement of African blacks, the concentration-camp displacement of the Nisei, or the destruction of the European Jewish community by the Nazi Holocaust. When the sudden, premature loss of innocence occurs within the totality of such overwhelming violations, the damaging consequences are usually catastrophic and lifelong. Fortunately, most children are safe from the devastation of such cataclysmic uprootings.

Most of the men and women who come to me for psychotherapy have *not* undergone such personal, social, or political catastrophes. Instead, their belief in fairy tales has been radically discredited by encounters with family hypocrisy. This totally contradicted what they had been taught to believe without allowing understanding of what was really going on.

While far less devastating than the total disruption brought about by political oppression, experiences such as these can be frightening and painfully confusing. They are often sufficiently damaging to make the victim feel unsafe about trusting others for a long, long time.

When the loss of innocence occurs too early or too suddenly but *in the absence* of family hypocrisy, the effects are short-lived. For example, a parent may unexpectedly let down a child, perhaps by breaking a promise. If this is acknowledged as a parental failing about which the child is entitled to his or her sadness and anger, the child may be expected to outgrow the resultant distrust and temporary grief that follows such disappointments.

In the presence of family hypocrisy, the child's illusions fall away to reveal the lies that the family lives. Any attempts by the child to point out the dishonesty of these discrepancies will be met with further denials and mystifications. It is one thing for a child to learn suddenly that the father whom he has been taught to respect and count on as a reliable provider is instead an undependable drunk. It is another for the parents to "explain" at that point that "daddy is just tired, and besides the doctor said that whiskey is a good tonic."

In the face of repeated experiences of overwhelming helplessness and bewilderment, the child must find a way to make sense of a confused and confusing world. There may be little option but to escape into the reassuring world of personal fantasies made up of variations on the disconcertingly discredited family fairy tales.

The raw sense of total vulnerability must be shielded. Increasingly, the child comes to depend on self-restricting, risk-avoiding, fantasy-bound attitudes and behaviors. These serve to deny threats to vulnerability by transforming the original authentic innocence into its caricature. Rollo May calls this "pseudo-innocence." [6] The pseudo-innocent denies his or her own power, identifies self-interest with the design of Providence, and pretends that this is the best of all possible worlds. Such a pose serves to deny feelings of hopelessness, makes the pain of disappointment more bearable, and brings a false sense of order to a chaotic life situation. The cost is high and unforeseen. These same defenses impoverish the possibilities for personal and spiritual growth that unfettered imagination and later life experiences might provide.

To survive emotionally, there may be little else such a child can do at the time. But out of such a configuration, the child gradually develops a neurotic way of life that continues on into adulthood. Pseudo-innocence requires wearing the blinders of denial. By making powerlessness into a seeming virtue, such a person acts as though God watches over the weak and the naïve. Preoccupation with the past involves pretending that, if childhood is never outgrown, one will always be watched over.

Residual weakness, helplessness, and dependency prevent people from ever feeling grown up. They remain embedded in nostalgic longing. It is not a matter of retaining childlike spontaneity but, rather of holding onto the childish insistence that someone else must take care of one so frail.

For others of us the dream of righteous vengeance maintains the image of heroic virtue as we await the time when we will be able to conquer all evil, to be recognized and appreciated at last. But it matters little whether the expectation of living happily ever after is sought through needless self-sorry suffering or by hazardously reckless romantic adventures. Feigned humility and pretended bravado bring the same results. The real dangers of life are obscured, the opportunities for growth overlooked, and the rewards of taking care of oneself missed.

Pseudo-innocence oversimplifies life by imposing unquestioned order on the arbitrariness of chance in each of our lives. By denying destructiveness in ourselves and others, it turns us toward easy and unwitting complicity with evil. Clinging to our insistence on perfection robs us of the power to take on that lifelong adult struggle between our ethical ideals and the imperfect situations with which we all must contend.

It is not the pain of disappointment alone that leads to neurotic pseudo-innocence. Suffering makes a child feel bad. It need not result in the self-destructive ways of living that come of clinging too long to illusions, nor to the anxiety and depression experienced when these illusions are threatened.

When Rollo May was doing research on *The Meaning of Anxiety,* he worked with a group of young unwed mothers in New York City.[7] This was during the 1940s when being single and pregnant was considerably more traumatic than it is now. May started out with the hypothesis that the predisposition to anxiety would be proportional to the degree of the subjects' rejection by their own mothers. Their difficult situation in this shelter for unwed mothers was expected to highlight the anxiety arising out of maternal rejection.

It turned out that half of the young women fit his hypothesis beautifully, while the other half did not fit at all. Every one of the women had suffered radical and painful rejection by her mother. However, there was one factor that differentiated the maternal rejection of the one group from that of the other. The women in the group with little anxiety and negligible neurotic patterns had been rejected *openly* and *honestly.*

May describes a woman, whom he chooses to call Helen, as the typical example of the low-anxiety, non-neurotic group:

[She] . . . was from a family of twelve children whose mother drove them out of the house on the first day of summer to stay with their father, the caretaker of a barge that went up and down the Hudson River. Helen was pregnant by her father. At the time she was in the shelter, he was in Sing Sing on a charge of rape by Helen's older sister. Like the other young women of this group, Helen would say . . . *"We have troubles, but we don't worry."* [8]

Helen's distinction is like that often attributed to the late Broadway producer Mike Todd, who was alleged to have said, "I've been broke lots of times, but I ain't never been poor." Trouble may be situational, but worry is always a state of mind. Accepting painful experiences openly and honestly eliminates needless suffering.

The loss of innocence is always painful, and grown-up acceptance of this inevitable transformation offers no guarantee that we will not fall on hard times again. But those of us who have had to deny our loss by willfully insisting on replacing the original state with pseudo-innocence are subject to anxiety and depression whenever this theatrical pose is in jeopardy. In addition to the chance blows to which life subjects everyone else, we add the needless suffering that comes from impossible demands that we be special, and that the world be fair and just.

2

Happily Ever After

Whenever childhood's core illusions are threatened by exposure to life as it is, the pseudo-innocent suffers the psychic pain of needless anxiety and depression. It is as though life without illusions would be totally unbearable.

That's a feeling I know well. For many years of my life I was stuck with such dread most of the time. Now I experience it less frequently, for briefer moments, and usually with less intensity. It occurs only when I absolutely refuse to surrender to recognizing myself as a responsible grown-up in a world that makes no sense. At such times I pay the high price of needless self-restriction and missed opportunities. But whatever the price of willfully clinging to my own fairy tales, occasionally it still seems to feel too awful to admit that I am just another ordinary guy living in a world that has no special plans for me.

It all started long ago in an unlikely setting for a tale of romantic ideals. Once upon a time in a small apartment in the Bronx. . . .

The fairy-tale atmosphere in which I grew up had three recurring motifs that made my life a very special one: (1) belonging to this family meant having blood-ties to people who could be counted on to take care of me even if no one else would; (2) belonging to the Jewish community offered the protection of "being with my own kind"; and (3) belonging to these parents held the promise that I could learn to be as good and honest as they were, and then live happily ever after.

I was part of a large family clan most of whom seemed to live right around the corner from one another. At first this felt reassuring. Presumably I always knew just where I stood within this "close" family. They loved me because of who I was (my mother's son). Though not a charter member, I had birthright status. I belonged. We even had a cousins' club.

Both my parents were the children of European immigrants. Each had many married brothers and sisters with children of their own. My father was one of nine, and my mother one of eleven. About once a month there was an engagement party, a wedding, a circumcision ceremony, a Bar Mitzvah, or a funeral. These small informal celebrations usually included only the immediate family, never less than a hundred people.

Only gradually did I begin to understand the complicated and conflicting configurations that underlay the reassuring slogans of family unity. My mother's parents had come to this country from Russia. Penniless, but filled with the hope of walking streets paved with gold, they arrived at Ellis Island on a cattleboat. Starting out from the familiar isolation of the *Stetl,* they ended up in the New World: living in a ghetto and working in a sweatshop.

My grandfather was described as a kindly old tailor. It took me a while to discover that after impregnating my grandmother sixteen times (there were five miscarriages), dear old grandpa had run off with some allegedly Christian, but otherwise unknown, younger woman.

The children remained loyal to grandma. For a long while I did not recognize how ashamed they felt of this "greenhorn" old lady who lived in America for thirty-five years without ever managing to learn to speak English. Though they supported her financially, they sometimes "had to" avoid her on the street when she appeared in public in her modified *Stetl* costume of housedress, slippers, and babushka, Americanized only by her unfortunate assimilation of wearing bobby socks.

Like many others of their generation, my parents had tried hard to become real Americans. Impatient Ellis Island immigration officials had shortened their peculiarly foreign last names. Individual siblings in turn changed their own too Jewish first names from Esther to Elizabeth, from Hannah to Anita, and from Chaim to Howard. All the family members of my parents' generation did their best to dress, talk, and act like "Yankees." My beleaguered grandmother could only mutter sardonically in Yiddish, "A blessing on Columbus."

My mother's oldest brother, Bill, was heir apparent. He took over as father surrogate after my grandfather deserted. Bill aspired to a career outside the sweatshop. Only the youngest brothers would have the opportunity to go to college. This possibility was never even considered for the sisters.

Still, without much formal education, Bill managed to move into the field of industrial advertising. Eventually, he published his own small directory of companies offering parts and services. This directory was distributed to manufacturers throughout the area. Taking on his two next younger brothers as assistants, he began to build a family micro-empire. As my mother and her many sisters married, their husbands were taken into the business as apprentices.

No sooner had the brothers-in-law learned how to run such an enterprise than they split off from the original family business to set up a competitive advertising directory of their own. Brutal internecine struggles followed, including ugly court fights with each faction attempting to have the other jailed for fraud, unfair business practices, and the like.

Once I became aware of these battles, I questioned the fairy-tale motif that we could always count on the family. I finally asked my mother, "But what about Uncle Bill?" Without missing a stroke, my mother answered: "My brother Bill is *not* family."

My father's side of the family also had a peculiarly marginal status. They remained too poor, sometimes went on welfare, and were unashamed of their lack of education. In addition, they were Hungarians. To me, they seemed more genuine, lusty, and just plain fun than my mother's side of the clan. But I learned to set them aside as poor (and therefore unworthy) relations. It all seemed very curious. We were fortunate in having a few well-off relatives from whom we could receive good quality hand-me-down clothing. My father's family was pathetic because they had to scrounge off us by accepting our hand-me-downs. It was clear that by "family" was meant only those relations on my mother's side who were in good standing at the time.

If I couldn't count on knowing who was family and who was not, at least I knew that I belonged to a Jewish community that would take care of me. Even there, the borders were sometimes fuzzy. For example, Uncle Jim was Italian. He had married my father's older sister, Ella. Jim was a sweet guy and a highly successful building contractor. As such, he was quite acceptable to the family. When I challenged my mother about Uncle Jim, she explained: "Italians are the same as Jews, *almost.*"

It was all very confusing. At fifteen, I fell in love with a girl of Italian-American descent. My folks were pleased to see me walking the neighborhood streets hand in hand with such a neat, clean, polite, and beautiful girl. Then they learned that her name was Nina Manuzza. Their response was to cut off my allowance, because "if you get involved with a Gentile, someday in the heat of argument, you get called Jew-Bastard."

My parents' apparent friendship with neighborhood first-generation American Jews added to my confusion. These neighbors were louder and more colorful than my parents. Publicly, my mother and father ignored these differences and treated our neighbors with politeness and kindness. Privately they referred to them as *Mockeys,* a Yiddish term referring to people who were "too Jewish." "They're the worst kind."

Nonetheless I believed that if I did what was called for in the Jewish community, I could still find a special place for myself. Earlier than was required, I announced that I wished to begin studying at the neighborhood synagogue's Hebrew School. This would mean giving up playtime three afternoons a week to learn the Hebrew language, customs, and rituals that would allow me to be confirmed at thirteen as a full member of the Jewish community in good standing.

My parents were delighted. Though they themselves never went to a synagogue except to participate in a family wedding or Bar Mitzvah, they considered it a blessing to have a son studying the Torah. Most important, I would learn enough Hebrew to be able to say *Kaddish,* the prayer for the dead. My parents would be remembered and honored even after they died.

I spent many tortured hours in the hot, sweaty back room of the synagogue, crowded in among other unhappy Jewish boys. It was clearly a matter of faith. What I remember most vividly is the pain of being rapped across the knuckles by the rabbi's metal-edged ruler when I made a mistake in my *Aleph, Beth, Gimel*s (the Hebrew A, B, Cs). Submitting voluntarily to this abuse is something I could only have suffered because I believed that it was the path toward my living happily ever after.

Getting up an hour early each morning, I would go through the ritual prayers, exercises, and ablutions. Not only was I going to be a good Jew, I was going to be the best Jew. One evening, after choosing to give up listening to Jack Armstrong and the Lone Ranger in order to do extra Hebrew study on my own at home, I announced to my parents that I had decided to become a rabbi. My mother's startled reply was, "What sort of a career is that for a nice Jewish boy?"

I treasured my *Siddur,* the ritual prayer book I had been given by the rabbi's wife, who was the real head of the Hebrew School. Knowing that this book must never touch the ground, and that it was so holy that it must eventually be burned rather than thrown away, I kept it on a special bookshelf-altar I had set aside for religious objects.

One morning, when I went to get this *Siddur* to say my prayers, I discovered that it was missing. I was frantic, but I dared not wake my parents so early. Praying (in English) that God would forgive me, I held off the ritual prayers until my parents awoke, thinking they might know what had become of my *Siddur.*

When I asked my father, he laughed. "Such a rattlebrained boy," he said. "You already forgot what you complained to me about last night. You whined that the little toy pool table I gave you for your birthday wasn't level. Didn't you think your father would take care of you? How come it didn't occur to you to look for your *Siddur* under the short leg of the pool table? Thank God, it was just the right size to level the table."

We did not observe any traditional Jewish religious practices at home. The one exception was the lighting of the *Jahrzeit,* a memorial anniversary candle for the dead . . . "just in case."

When my parents first married, my mother had put a great deal of energy into observing the elaborate kosher dietary rules so that my grandmother would feel comfortable eating at our house.

Grandma sometimes visited, but she never trusted my mother enough to accept anything but a cup of black coffee. In disgust, my mother eventually gave up trying to "keep kosher."

When I set out to change all of this, my parents seemed to encourage me. I remember the first time I was advanced enough in my Hebrew studies to be able to conduct the lighting of the Hanukkah candles. My parents seemed very proud as they watched and listened as I lit the candles in ritual fashion, chanting the required blessings to complete the ceremony. Then we all sat down to eat. It turned out that my mother was serving *ham* steaks for supper!

There were curious twistings and turnings to the family's religious hypocrisy. Though the high holiday of Yom Kippur (the Day of Atonement) required day-long synagogue attendance and fasting, we participated in none of the penitent behavior by which a Jew examines his or her behavior of the past year in order to turn toward being a better person during the year ahead.

One of the small indulgences to be sacrificed during that time is smoking. On that day, my parents smoked, but only in the house. By the time I was old enough to smoke, I had given up ritual religious practices. On Yom Kippur I too was permitted to smoke at home, but not on the streets. I could not understand this arbitrary distinction until my parents explained: "To be a good Jew does not mean that you have to follow every silly little rule like a greenhorn (immigrant). But to smoke in the street on Yom Kippur is an offense to the community. You don't have to follow the rules, but you must never spit in God's eye."

One after another, the illusions dissolved. Family was sometimes not family. It seemed almost impossible to figure out what it meant to be Jewish. I felt that I had only one hope left. If I could learn to be as good and as honest as my parents, then things would surely work out well for me.

Some of the pieces of that fairy tale had also crumbled early. I had been told that I was not yet good enough to live right, so for a time I could expect to continue to get into trouble again and again. Not to worry. If I would only come to my parents and confess to whatever mischief I had been into this time, they would understand. They would not be angry, and I would not be punished.

The earliest confession I can remember was of stealing change out of my mother's purse. I wanted to do something terribly important at the time. The local movie theater had a Saturday afternoon special consisting of a great double feature, a Flash Gordon serial installment, cartoons, door prizes . . . the works. I was nine. I was also broke.

Stealing money that first time was a great adventure. The movie show was all the more marvelous because I had almost missed seeing it. But by that evening I felt unbearably burdened by having had to endure for a full hour and a half the guilt of a nine-year-old who had so enjoyed spending the stolen fifteen cents' worth of his parents' hard-earned money. I determined to throw off that burden at suppertime. It was the soonest that I could find my parents together. Even though it was a terrible crime and engendered a great deal of guilt, a single confession seemed sufficient to me.

I was smart enough to start out by telling my folks what a wonderful matinee show the local movie house had been offering, how much I had wanted to see it, and how sad I had felt about not being able to afford to go. Next I played back their sermonette: no matter what I might have done wrong, if only I told the truth, they would not get angry, and I would not get punished. They assured me that I understood correctly how it was in our family about getting into trouble, not lying about it, and all that.

Then I made the mistake of telling the truth about having taken the fifteen cents out of my mother's pocketbook. Before I could go on to say just how sorry I was, and how somehow I would make it up to them, my mother reached across the table and smacked me full in the face. "Our son is a thief!" she shouted at my father. As instructed, he took over. Speaking to her, rather than to me, he offered the absolute assurance: "He will never steal again. No movies for the rest of the summer."

Needless to say, I did steal again. But I didn't steal to get movie money. Within two weeks my father was slipping me fifteen cents each Saturday morning, saying, "Go enjoy the movies, but don't tell your mother. I don't want her to be upset with *you*."

I could see then that the honesty of my confession was not sufficient. It could not make up for my initial dishonesty in stealing in the first place. If I could learn to be as basically honest as my parents, only then could any minor flaws in my character be overcome by my truthfulness about them.

I was a few years older when this fairy tale went the way of the first two, and my primary innocence along with it. It was my fourteenth summer. School was out and I had not yet been able to get a vacation job. My mother was afraid that having unsupervised time and nothing to do, as always I would certainly get into trouble. She instructed my father to take me along with him each morning when he went downtown to his office.

The idea was for me to learn something useful about honest labor. Dutifully, my father took me along. For the most part, he left me in one of the empty rooms to play with a typewriter and an adding machine, and to learn to string paper clips. Soon bored, I began to wander around. My father decided it was time to teach me something about the advertising business.

The firm had been set up by two of my uncles who were married to my mother's sisters. My father had had an opportunity to join in the partnership when the firm was founded, but declined because he did not want to take on the exploitive role of being a boss. Instead he had taken on the martyr role of an exploited employee.

My two uncles had combined their last names to come up with a title for the firm and its publication. The result was "a happy accident." The name of their firm sounded very much like the name used by the telephone company's advertising directory. Because they both liked the color, they had also chosen to print their own directory on remarkably similar *yellow pages.*

My father wore two hats. He was manager of the home office during the compilation, layout, and actual publication of the directory. Much of the rest of the year he was on the road, moving from one industrial city to another as manager of an advertising-space sales crew. He had already told me that it was a "tricky" business because what they sold was *space* in the directory. "And what is space?" he would go on. "Space is nothing. That's our product, nothing. It's not easy to sell nothing."

That summer at the office he showed me one of the ways that "nothing" could be sold by mail. He had two clerical workers going through out-of-town telephone company directories. Under his supervision, they would locate and clip out "boxes and cap listings" for industrial service and product firms. The boxed ads and the listings in capital letters were the only ones for which these firms had to pay the telephone company.

The clipped ads and listings from the telephone directory were then pasted onto "Renewal Forms" for ads in the directory for which my father worked. The fine print at the bottom of the form acknowledged that the ad in question had *originally* been published in the telephone company's directory.

The busy industrial executives to whom these forms were mailed would need to take the time to read them very carefully. Otherwise these "customers" would certainly believe that they were simply contracting for renewal of their already purchased space in the Yellow Pages of the telephone directory.

Once I understood how this worked, I got very upset. I asked my father to join me in the empty office so that I could talk to him privately. "Dad, I don't understand what's going on here. This seems dishonest. It's like stealing."

"You're just too young to understand," he reassured me. "This isn't dishonest, and it's certainly not stealing. It's just *kuchel-muchel.*"

No matter how many times we talked about it after that, I could never get anyone in the family to give me a literal translation of *kuchel-muchel.* The clearest it became was that this was a Jewish version of hocus-pocus, just a matter of "good business sense" and no more. My mother's added clarification was, "Your father is completely honest. It's just that every *man* has a little larceny in his heart."

That made three for three. The fairy tale of family unity had been exposed as shifting and unreliable. The hope of becoming a member of a Jewish community that would take care of me was too filled with contradictions to count on. And now the promise of a good life based on being as honest as my parents turned out to be a deception.

If only someone had said to me, "We misled you. Real life is not the fairy tale we made it out to be." But instead I was told that all the family fairy tales were still true. I was instructed to ignore the contradictions. Even if it meant denying the evidence of my experience and the confirmation of my feelings, I was to go on pretending that we were not pretending.

I could no longer tell what was real and what wasn't. I only knew that I was confused and that my parents were no longer to be trusted. I was as yet too helpless and bewildered to try to take on a world that made no sense.

The terror of feeling that vulnerable was too overwhelming to be faced squarely. In a desperate attempt to cling to the remnants of my shattered innocence, I developed fairy tales of my own. Unwittingly, I gradually created the myth of myself as superadequate loner, an errant-knight who would go my own way, needing nothing from anyone else as I righted the wrongs of an unjust world. Outrageously reckless, I challenged every windmill along the way. Eventually I no longer needed a family. I didn't need anyone. Though others might not yet be aware of it, it was they who needed me.

The religion of my parents was no longer meaningful to me. My last bit of participation in Jewish ritual was having a Bar Mitzvah on my thirteenth birthday. After that day, I never again entered a synagogue as a participant. By middle adolescence, I had converted to the secular faiths of social reform and militant atheism.

At first my crusade was a commitment to "cross-cultural encounter" (translation: I would not date Jewish girls). Later I became a "Negrophile." My original interest in Jewish culture had been transformed into marginal anti-Semitism. All the positive feelings were transferred onto my romanticized image of Negro culture. As a late adolescent, I enlarged my interest in jazz and integration into that proud, righteous valor of being the noble half of an interracial couple. I dated black women, hung around Harlem, was often the only white at otherwise black parties, and made an altogether patronizing pest of myself.

I dealt with the discredited fairy tale of family honesty by developing the fantasy that I could see the truth where others could not. My deluded self-image became that of a totally honest human being, perhaps the only one. I most often corroborated this fantasy by insisting on saying whatever I was thinking, mindless of the ways it might hurt other people or get me in trouble. Truth was my flaming sword. I assured myself that other people did not like me only because I was too honest for them.

As for making money, I was above such worldly concerns. Too long, I worked for two dollars an hour as a clinical psychologist at a monolithic state mental institution. I was ready to sacrifice those things that had been so important to my parents. I wanted only the opportunity to free oppressed inmates from the ogres who held them captive.

It was a time of much heat, a time of little light. Boldly I struggled and nobly I suffered. I accomplished little of any real worth to others, but what can you expect from so young a hero? In time I would show them. Someday *everyone* would appreciate what I was trying to do for them.

In the meantime, I suffered needlessly. Everyone must endure life's misfortunes. As a pseudo-innocent, I was a double sufferer, afflicted not only by the real world but by my fantasies as well. It now seems too a high price to pay for retaining the illusion of heroic adventure.

3

The Heroic Adventurer

As a pseudo-innocent, I clung to a fairy-tale vision of the world. I believed that my own life story was to have a beginning, a middle, and a happy ending. There would be major and minor characters, good guys and bad guys, with myself cast as the central protagonist. As the hero, there would be tests I must pass and lessons I must learn before receiving the just rewards for my show of courage and acquisition of wisdom.

I saw my professional career as a natural path for the heroic adventure I had in mind. Early on, I did what I could to maintain the fantasy that I was becoming a Merlin, possessor of secret wisdom and practitioner of white magic. At the same time I played at being Lancelot, nobly committed to rescuing the victims of ogres, witches, and evil stepmothers.

At that time, it was *I* who sought out the patients from among the captive populations of public institutions. Some of them did what they could to instruct me about the need to lose my pseudo-innocence. It was not yet time for me to begin to face the world as it is so that I might get on with my real work. My education took longer than it might have. Not that these patients were inept teachers. It was just that, like all pseudo-innocents, I was a slow learner. I stubbornly ignored any hard facts of experience that threatened to disrupt the reassuring comfort of my wishful fantasies.

I remember when I began work at the New Jersey State Psychiatric Hospital at Trenton. The institution was made up of great old stone buildings set in open fields, and connected by pleasant tree-shaded paths. The main gate was situated on *Asylum* Road.

I was very pleased with myself. First day on the job and already I felt like an important member of the professional staff. As I strolled the institution grounds, white-uniformed nurses offered starched, clean, and courteous greetings. Though I had not yet completed my doctoral studies, I accepted their undeserved heralding of "Good morning, Doctor."

It was just the sort of sparkling, sunny day that fit my sense of being the right man in the right place. It was the first day of my new life. I had made a wise choice in securing permission to tour on my own the building in which I was to work my magic. Following the personnel director's overly detailed directions, I spotted the huge weeping willow that marked the road I was to follow.

At the foot of the tree, I could see a signpost. It was still too far off for me to be absolutely sure that I was on the right path. Hurrying on, I got close enough to the wooden sign to read the Old English lettering of its cracked and peeling paint. The inscription assured me of my progress: TO THE BUILDING FOR THE CRIMINALLY INSANE. As I approached the turn-off, I was thrown off stride by a second sign. Smaller and several inches below the first, the raised black-and-white letters of this traffic marker read DEAD END ROAD.

I stopped short in momentary panic, suddenly not knowing which path to follow. Squaring my shoulders, I turned myself in the direction indicated by the signs and began a determined march toward the building. Walking confidently once more, I followed the long, winding road. At first I was only dimly aware of the great gray stones of the fortress to which the road led. Yet already I felt very much like a mounted knight on the way to single-handed storming of the castle of the evil baron. It was all I could do to suppress the urge to click my tongue, slap my hip, and gallop down the path as I had so often as a boy.

Bringing an intentional show of quiet dignity to my walk, I moved more slowly toward the sunlit building on which I now concentrated my gaze. Uneasily I noted the contrasting harshness of its surrounding barbed-wire-topped enclosure. Examining more carefully the place in which I was to work, I became aware of another disappointing detail. A few minutes earlier the sunlight's glinting had turned my distant destination into a magic castle. Closer up, the far-off gleaming was transformed into the building reflection of the steel-barred windows of a modernized maximum-security prison. The unintentional effect made the grim structure grimmer still.

My high mood was jarred by the onslaught of all this unexpected reality. Reaching into the inner breast pocket of my carefully tailored tweed jacket, I took out a brand-new handsomely tooled leather cigarette case. I smiled to myself, warmed by the memory of the gift card that it still contained. The card read: "Carry this token of my love as you brave this new adventure. Marjorie."

Taking a cigarette from the fresh pack, I lit it with the intention of taking time out for a slow relaxing smoke. Instead, I found that I smoked quickly and nervously, impatiently tossing away the butt as I bounded up the several worn stone steps of the building. I was halted by a large, closed steel door. In many places the paint had been scratched away to reveal heart-shaped areas of shiny metal that enclosed the initials of former visitors and their imprisoned lovers.

I looked in vain for a knob or a doorhandle. There was none. Testily, I pushed at the heavy metal door but I couldn't budge it. Growing suddenly frantic, I was about to hammer on the door with my fists. Then I noticed a small tarnished brass plaque commanding me to RING HERE. I followed instructions and pushed the large, cracked, black button below the metal plate. The momentary Alice-in-Wonderland atmosphere was dissipated by a dull metallic clatter from beyond the door.

After waiting longer than seemed necessary, I heard the reluctant sound of shuffling feet and idly clanking brass. Through the small wire-enforced thick glass window, I saw the irritated smile of the white-uniformed keeper of the lock. As if to prove that it had not been forgotten, he held his clanking instrument up to the shatter-proof window. I couldn't tell whether it was a doorhandle that doubled as a key, or a key that also served as a doorhandle.

He waited for my begrudging nod of acknowledgment before inserting his cranklike key-doorhandle into the lock. Through the narrow waist-high slots in the door came his muffled, "Comin' right up, Doc." When he finally opened the door, the attendant continued to bar my entrance, challenging, "You got an identification card, Doc? Regulations, you know. We gotta be strict. This is a powderkeg of a building."

"Certainly, right here," I answered, holding out the newly typed card that the personnel director had issued to me only minutes earlier. "You have your job to do, and I have mine. My name is Kopp. That's K-O-P-P. I'm the new assistant to the chief psychologist, Dr. Perry. I'm going to assist in the treatment of sex offenders here."

The attendant seemed singularly unimpressed. "Yeah, well, my name's Charlie Macken. Do you really think you can cure them sex fiends, Doc?" Without waiting for an answer, he turned and started across the reception area.

Alone, I made my way toward the next barred threshold. The double-grill gates enclosed an eight-by-ten-foot limbo. They were never to be opened at the same time. A visitor must pass through the first one and have it closed and locked behind him before the second was opened.

I pressed the button that sounded a buzzer inside "the cage," the little room in which the attendant sat. From his sheltered perch, this guardian looked out through a reinforced window onto the area between the grill gates. Magnifying mirrors, angled up into the corners of this enclosure, allowed him to see those who awaited his services.

Having received a confirming hand signal from Charlie, he threw the lever that opened the first gate. I stepped through. The gate clanked shut behind me, shutting off my retreat. I felt as though *I* was in a cage. After what seemed an awfully long time, the inner gate opened before me. I found myself released onto a long, poorly lit corridor. Noticing the familiar examining and staff-meeting rooms, I felt my confidence restored. I sauntered down the hall, looking over the physical plant.

At the end of the corridor was another locked heavy metal door. I pushed the buzzer. Flashing my pass to the next attendant when he peered through the small window, I was admitted to a vast hexagonal room. Directly across this open area was a large, high-ceilinged, painfully unadorned diningroom. The endless rows of plain wooden tables and benches made it look like a movie set for a Jimmy Cagney film. At the moment it was empty except for a clean-up detail.

This attendant was older and more friendly than the others. To my right and left, locked passageways emanated from the hexagonal center room in which he stood. "That's why they call it 'the Star,'" he volunteered. "We control much of the population's movements from here."

Feeling that I'd finally found a genuinely cooperative guide, I said with assurance, "I'd like to see a typical patient living-area, if I may."

"Well, some men sleep in dormitories, others in cells, and some in sickrooms. We also have a library, a recreation yard, a dayroom, and of course the shops the men work in. Just where would you like to begin, Doctor?"

"I don't have time to go all through the building today. Supposing I start with the sickroom corridor. You needn't trouble to do anything more than let me in."

There was a subtle change in the tone of voice of the smiling attendant. "You're the doctor, Doctor." Shaking his head, he admitted me to the corridor beyond the locked door on my far right.

As soon as the door banged closed behind me, I realized that I'd made a mistake. In all the other institutions in which I'd worked and consulted, sickrooms housed the physically ill. Here in the building for the criminally insane, it was clear that they had been reserved for the more seriously mentally disturbed patients, and probably for the incorrigible troublemakers as well.

The long, dark, crowded corridor was unevenly patched with sunlight coming through the barred windows high on the right-hand wall. It was the sun's reflections from these same windows that had lent enchantment to my initially hazy view of the far-off building. On the left was a row of doors to the "sickrooms." The euphemism masked individual cells each crudely furnished with a metal cot; a single heavy, wooden, armless chair; a tiny table; and a built-in, smelly, seatless toilet.

My image of a familiar sickroom corridor had no place for patients such as these. Unattended by any staff member, many sprawled listlessly on the cement floor, backs propped against the stone walls and legs outstretched. Some huddled together, whispering in conspiratorial tones.

At the far end of the hallway a larger group was noisily horsing around, the sound of their coarse voices punctuated by outbursts of raucous laughter. Still others roamed the corridor in seemingly endless, aimless search, gesticulating crazily to invisible companions with whom they shared their mad secrets.

Suddenly I remembered that I had not yet set up my office. It now seemed to me that I might not really have time enough to make my way down the body-littered corridor. After all, it was my first day at the institution and there were other places yet to be seen. I half-turned toward the locked door through which I had entered a few moments earlier.

My opportunity for decision was preempted. Feeling a clawlike grip on my arm, I turned quickly to find myself staring into the gray-stubbled face of a strange little spider-crab of a man. In spite of myself, I felt repelled by the grip of his scrawny, wrinkled hand on my newly pressed jacket. But the terror in his eyes would not permit me to abandon him.

"What is it you want?" I asked more harshly than I intended. Then more gently, "Is there something I can do for you?"

The old man cackled at having taken me captive. He spoke in a frightened staccato whisper, "We must save ourselves. You've only just come in time. Together we might be able to escape."

"Now you wait a minute . . . ," I began, remembering a newspaper account of rioting prison inmates murdering their hostages. Then looking at this pathetically withered character, I felt foolish. "I'm sorry, old man, but—"

"Not so blasted loud," the old man interrupted, grasping at the lapels of my jacket. "If he should hear you, we're done for, and that's no fairy tale."

"All right, all right," I found myself whispering. I freed my lapels from his grip only to have him take my arm once more and stealthily lead me down the hallway. We stepped over the outstretched legs of seated patients, but the old man continued to act as though we were alone.

"He's been after me and my family for years," he went on. "It's always us that has position and wealth that are the targets of such varlets. It's the cross the landed gentry has always had to bear. Nobility suffers the same you know."

"I know, oh I do know," I answered, falling in with the game. There appeared little else I could do. "But tell me, just who is it that's behind all this?"

The old man looked around suspiciously before daring to reveal the plot. After somehow reassuring himself, he confided, "It's Tic Tac Tannenbaum, the Trenton Triggerman."

That did it. I'd had enough. If I'd been offered an international espionage ring, or the Third Man, or even Robin Hood I might have gone on listening. But this improbably alliterative allegation was just too much.

Disengaging myself as gently as possible I said, "Well, you just tell your regular doctor about all that when he comes by. I'm sure he'll try to help you."

To my surprise, the old man reached up and pulled on both of his ears as if in some secret lodge sign. Somehow satisfied with my response, he winked merrily and sneaked off back down the corridor.

Finding myself halfway down the hall already, I decided to go on after all. Most of the seated patients simply ignored me. I observed them carefully, making mental notes. The old man had been a paranoid schizophrenic or perhaps an advanced case of central nervous system syphilis. I planned to find out his name and check his diagnosis. Looking around I picked out a catatonic, rolled up in an intra-uterine ball, and an agitated depressive pacing back and forth, wringing his hands, with tears streaming down his cheeks. The truth of things was beginning to fall into place.

I walked on down the hallway with a renewed sense of knowing what I was about. A tall, rangy, bull-chested man in his early twenties detached himself from one of the smaller knots of patients. Stepping into the center of the corridor, he folded his arms and planted himself directly in my path. With legs spread wide apart, he began slowly rocking back and forth on the balls of his feet.

I slowed my pace but did not stop. I couldn't run and I certainly didn't want to fight. What was I thinking of? I was the doctor and this was a patient.

For a moment the threatened confrontation had taken me back to the anti-Semitic challenges I had to face as a kid when I dared to take a shortcut home through the forbidden Gentile neighborhoods.

I had rarely run away and had often gotten pushed around. Though I was supposed to try to avoid fights, I was never to deny that I was a Jew. It was a curiously passive, stuck-feeling kind of courage.

Now I had a duty to perform that paralleled that early paradox. I was there to help. I could not set aside my identity as a therapist. This very man who now menaced me might later be in therapy as my patient. Yet no Gentile ever had seemed more foreign than this obviously criminal type who had thrown down the gauntlet. I became aware that other patients were silently watching to see whether or not I would pick it up.

My opponent did not move. Carried more by inertia than by decision I continued stiffly but steadily down the corridor. The patient's face grew tense behind his derisive smile. My guts knotted in response, but still I went on, knowing it was already too late to retreat.

I found myself within inches of that bull-chest and still moving. I was about to collide when his expression shifted to a broader "aw shucks" sort of a grin. Stepping aside with exaggerated politeness, he spoke out in mock bewilderment, "Oh, did you want to get through here, Doc?"

My fear gave way to relief, then to irritation at having been taken in. When my emotional outlook eased into a more good-humored silent laugh at myself, I finally answered, "Yes, thanks."

Several of the other patients crowded around us, laughing and pushing at one another. They seemed very interested in me.

"Are you the new doctor on the staff?" asked one.

"Will you be working here in this building, Doc?" another inquired.

Then a third entreated, "How about a cigarette, huh, Doc? It's tough getting tailor-mades in here."

Still another explained, "Yeah, we roll our own, like Gene Autry. Got one for me, too?"

"We sure need more doctors on the staff."

Flattered and relieved by this new air of recognition and respect, I opened my leather cigarette case to the first man who asked.

"Hey, nice case. Look, you guys," he said admiringly. I hardly noticed that he had taken the case from my hand and passed it on.

Now it was my turn to keep them in suspense by indulging the position provided by my anonymity. "Well, for now let's just say I'm a new doctor and let it go at that. You'll find out all the rest in a few days. Now that's not so long to wait, is it?"

The man who had challenged me answered for the group. "Okay, Doc, we can wait. Can't we guys? You know these doctors. We can't find out a thing unless they want us to know."

It felt finished for now. "I've about done what I came for. I'm going to leave now, but I'll be coming back to get to know you men better."

"Let's get out of the Doc's way," the young leader commanded. The others backed off to let me through. "Don't forget your cigarette case," he said to me. "It's really a beaut."

His honesty and respect gave me as much pleasure as the actual return of the treasured case. It would have been a real prize in a place like this. I knew that this transaction would go a long way in establishing me as an accepted professional who knew how to handle difficult situations.

Warm smiles were exchanged as I said goodbye. Confidently, I headed back toward the door through which I had entered so uncertainly a few minutes earlier. Halfway there I paused to open my cigarette case. It now seemed like a genuine talisman. The case felt lighter than it should have. My hands trembled involuntarily as I opened it. The case was *empty*.

For a moment I shook my head in bewilderment. When I entered the building, it had contained an almost full pack of cigarettes. Now there was nothing in it except Marjorie's gift card. As I turned, the jeering laughter of the group reached my ears. They were all smoking with great affectation, puffing great clouds of smoke into the air, and fingering the unlit prizes each had tucked behind his ear.

I was no longer bewildered. Almost before they'd begun their taunting catcalls, I knew that I'd been had.

"Hey, *Mister* Doctor, how you gonna bug out the sex class if you can't even hold onto your smokes?"

"Yeah, man, if you're such a big-shot psychologist, how come they didn't have your office ready for you?"

"And if you're gonna be Doc Perry's number two man, why ain't he here to meet you?"

I felt twice the fool. While letting me believe that I was in command of the situation, they had taken me in by beating me out of my cigarettes. Now they had turned my cloak of anonymity into a set of emperor's new clothes. I could feel the heat rising in my cheeks and spreading to my ears. I blushed uncontrollably at the humiliation I felt.

They knew things about me they couldn't possibly have known. The inmate grapevine. I'd seen it in the movies and had scoffed at this romantic belief in the powers of the criminal mind. Right now it all seemed very real.

Hoping to show them that I was a good sport, I mustered a weak and unconvincing smile. They went right on jeering.

Abruptly, I turned and began the long walk back down the crowded sickroom corridor. I tried to appear casual as I stumbled over the outstretched legs of one patient and bumped squarely into another. Reaching the locked door, I paused so that they could see that I was in no great hurry to leave.

Just as I raised my hand to push the button that would summon the attendant, I heard it. The voice belonged to the bull-chested young tough. Its taunting singsong lilt easily bridged the long corridor between us. "Be sure to tell Marjorie about your latest adventure."

I felt as though I wanted to kill him. If I turned I knew I would attack my bull-chested tormenter, attack wildly, stupidly, and defeatedly. My hand shook with tension, but somehow my finger found the button and pushed it. By the time I reached the other side of the door, my rage had turned to shame.

Waiting for the attendant at each gate was even more difficult than it had been when I entered. Hardly hearing their comments, I did not look up when they spoke.

After what seemed like a long, long time, I was outside in the late morning sunshine once more, walking the tree-shaded paths, walking fast. The whole escapade seemed a little less real out where free men walked. As the sharply cutting edges of the experience dulled in the open air, I began to see that the main thing was not to lose my head. After all, it had been no more than an isolated incident, born of my relative unfamiliarity with the criminal mind. Nothing more. It was easily rectified. I had only to read up on the subject. Armed with newly acquired wisdom, I would return in triumph.

4

The Magic Helper

Fixated on his or her own childhood, the nostalgia of the pseudo-innocent pivots on the wish to make things work out right once and for all. "It's just not fair" is the anguished outcry. This is not an understandable protest against social or political injustice. Rather, it is a self-absorbed petulant insistence on the right to an unpromised rose garden, or at the very least a demand for restitution for an unfortunate personal accident of birth.

Imagining themselves to be the heroes or heroines of as yet uncompleted fairy tales, such people simply cannot (will not) believe that the villains who have disappointed them will go unpunished, or that they themselves will remain blameless yet uncompensated victims. Surely there must be someone who will avenge them and take good care of them, someone who will right the family wrongs and reward the good children.

Those of us who are caught up in these romantic fantasies go on insisting that there must be someone who will mend our broken childhood dreams. We long to participate in caretaking relationships. In our search for such a magic helper, some of us become psychotherapy patients. A few of us even presume that we ourselves can become magic helpers. So it is that some of us go on to become psychotherapists.

There are hazards to either course.

At a conscious, rational level the unhappy person who consults a psychotherapist is simply a patient seeking expert professional help for the purpose of getting relief from neurotic symptoms. At a less-conscious fantasy level, what he or she is seeking is other fairy-tale characters: a Prince Charming, a Merlin, or perhaps a Fairy Godmother. The real danger lies in finding one.

Unfortunately there are psychotherapists whose own hidden pseudo-innocent beliefs include imagining themselves being exactly the sort of magic helper that such a patient has been seeking. Such pairings constitute therapeutic misalliances within which the fantasies of both partners may be acted out. Unwittingly they collude to avoid discovering that they are only ordinary people living matter-of-fact lives in an indifferent world that has no special plans for satisfactory conclusions to any of our randomly ordered lives.

When we decide to become psychotherapists, consciously we see ourselves as making a vocational choice of entering one of the socially sanctioned helping professions. On an unconscious level there is always more to it. No one becomes a psychotherapist with a clear idea of what he or she is getting into. At first few of us realize how presumptuous it is to put ourselves in the position of guiding other people in solving their life problems. All of us have hidden irrational motives for first choosing to become psychotherapists.

Some of us wish to cure our crazy families. Others seek a vicarious path to self-understanding. Most of us want to become that magic helper we once needed. If only such a helper had appeared to take care of us when we were helplessly confused unhappy children, we could have lived happily ever after.

For the first few years of practice, the therapist lives out the illusions that first led to his or her choosing to practice this folk art. Only as these illusions are gradually given up do more realistic motivations emerge. It is these more mature reasons for doing the work that serve the patient best. Time is a necessary if not sufficient condition for their development.

> To be a poet at twenty is to be twenty.
> But to be a poet at forty is to be a poet.[1]

Though some of us have worked through or otherwise outgrown a large measure of our pseudo-innocence, we psychotherapists continue to live out certain implicit fairy-tale motifs. Much of contemporary psychotherapy has its roots in psychoanalysis. In our work we retain a covert psychoanalytic doctrine that continues to account for many of our professional miseries. Despite Freud's own acceptance of the inevitability of human frailty, many later psychotherapists remain enchanted with a hidden belief in the *perfectibility of human beings.* This quest after the impossible dream creates failures where we might otherwise have successes, and anguish where we might otherwise experience joy.

When questioned individually, we each seem to know better. Any seasoned psychotherapist would quickly acknowledge that this is a seriously flawed life in which an amalgam of compromises is the best that any of us can hope for. No matter how expert the therapy, no patient can be totally freed from the destructive effects of a particularly brutal or premature loss of original innocence. The scars of early traumatic experiences never fully heal. In protecting old wounds we are all capable of acting in irrationally defensive ways that do not now serve our best interests.

Still the way we therapists proceed with our "talking cure" makes clear that at some level we believe that magic words can make people happy, and that the truth can make them free. Leslie Farber unmasks this heretical doctrine of the attainment of purity when he writes sardonically:

. . . however rarely the goal of perfection may be achieved, man is a creature who is, nonetheless, psychologically perfectible, by virtue of either the early and happy accident of childhood or the later and unhappy necessity of psychoanalysis.[2]

Many therapists believe that diagnosis is the first step in the work of correcting the condition that prevents the patient from living happily ever after. Torrey has termed this the "Rumpelstiltskin Principle." [3] Most of us remember that lovely fairy tale by the Brothers Grimm.

After pretending to take care of the queen by fulfilling her impossible obligation of spinning a roomful of flax into gold, that evil dwarf demanded that she give up her baby in return for his help. No need to worry! In fairy tales there is always a way to make things right. If only the queen could guess the dwarf's name, she could save her baby. Though she tried and tried, the queen could not come up with that magic word.

Time was running out. There seemed to be no solution to her terrible problem. Then one night she followed the dwarf to his secret cottage in the woods. From a hidden place, she spied him dancing around a fire singing to himself:

> Spinning flax is my game
> And Rumpelstiltskin is my name.

As soon as she learned to call him by his right name, the queen was able to save her baby. She and the princess lived happily ever after.

In making diagnoses, we therapists use the Rumpelstiltskin Principle by naming the patient's overall problem. The patient's anxiety is immediately somewhat decreased by having found a magic helper who is wise enough to know what's wrong.

The therapeutic effect of that naming process is expanded in the exploration that follows. The therapist listens carefully and observes the patient until it is possible to begin to make "correct interpretations." By giving meaning to apparently meaningless sequences of thoughts and behaviors, the therapist can begin to name the patient's secret wishes.

By accepting the magic of the therapist's words, the patient gradually gains "insight" into his or her problems. This understanding gives the patient power over the forces of darkness (the unconscious) that have created the needless (neurotic) suffering.

All of this word-magic is performed within the context of exploring the patient's past. Attachment to the past, whether vengeful or nostalgic, is believed to prevent happiness in the present. The patient tells his or her story in order to find out how badly it *begins*. Both the therapist and the patient believe that the story must *end* well if only they first go through the called-for corrective word-magic together.

Most often this return to the patient's beginnings unearths the painful memories of having been raised by bad parents. It turns out that the patient was a good child who loved the ogre and the witch. In treating this innocent child so unfairly, it is as though the villainous pair cast an evil spell that has resulted in the patient's continuing neurotic unhappiness.

The patient longs for the good parent, hoping to find this magic helper in the person of the therapist. If the therapist loves the patient who suffers from feelings of inferiority, the spell will be broken. The frog will become a handsome prince once more. If the therapist gives the inadequate patient the magic sword of personal power, the patient will be able to avenge all the wrongs of the world. One magic kiss on the cheek of Sleeping Beauty will surely awaken the depressed patient to the joys of living.

Too often these fairy-tale solutions are the core of the therapist's fantasies as well. One trainee in my supervisory seminar was treating a female patient whom he hugged at the end of every session. He had no clear memory of what they talked about during the hour. That didn't much matter, he explained. It was the hug that *she* came for each week. His caring about her was all that would be needed to make her life happier!

We therapists often view the patient as having been scapegoated by his or her family. In family therapy, we speak of the *identified patient,* the symptomatic member who has been exploited into being the repository of everyone else's problems. This diagnosable innocent victim is often our favorite in that family.

In this way the therapist becomes involved in the willful romance that sometimes passes for a therapeutic relationship. Again and again I find myself falling into the error of white-knighting [4] my own patients. Whenever I live out the fairy tale of being the magic helper, I am tempted to cast the patient as the scapegoat of a bad family. In contrast to these evildoers who have treated my patient so unfairly, I am the totally accepting parent of this innocent child/adult.

At such times I cannot see how either the patient or I could have contributed in any way to our own difficulties. Together we can live out a pseudo-innocent alliance that bolsters our belief that we are special. Mistakenly, we view ourselves and each other as totally helpless victims of our pasts. Paradoxically, at the same time, we envision ourselves becoming the triumphantly powerful masters of our futures.

Again and again these transference and countertransference fantasies must be discredited as we struggle toward living life as the ordinary people we both turn out to be. We must come to live within the shifting ambiguities of being both good and bad, wise and foolish, fortunate and unfortunate.

As the more experienced patient of the two, I most often take the lead in recognizing the fanciful mess we have gotten into. At times the actual patient is clearer about the ways in which we have been fooling each other and ourselves. In either case, we both must continue our lifelong struggles against the temptation to maintain our ultimately unrewarding pseudo-innocent postures. How can we depend on one another without expecting to be taken care of? When is it wise to trust the other, with what, and how much? What is the best way for each of us to manage his or her finally unmanageable life?

This book emerged out of my own lifelong search for answers to these questions. In it I have attempted to reveal pieces of my own too-early loss of innocence, my desperate attempts to shield my vulnerability with vengeful distrust, and my learning to risk trusting once more, sometimes. As always, this writing is my way of continuing to do the needed work on my self. I have no doubt but that in trying to outgrow my remaining pseudo-innocence in this way, unwittingly I reveal how I still cling to it.

Many of the men and women who come to me for psychotherapy are also struggling against the painful impact of their own lost innocence. Some cling hysterically to the useless remnants of childhood illusions. They depend on the forced optimism of denial to make their pain disappear. Others seem to have given up hope, trust, and all chance of adult fulfillment. They fight off their longings with obsessive doubt, with paranoid cynicism, or with the pessimism of depression. My accounts and explorations in this book derive from my work with these patients and from my personal life, out of their struggles and my own.

The loneliness of my own youthful loss of innocence was made bearable partly by the supportive instruction that I received from reading other people's tales of their inevitable fall from grace. As in my earlier writings, I have here regathered some of the tales that helped me, so that others may see what I saw. Together we may yet learn how to bear being on our own as grown-ups in an unjust world in which there is no one else to take care of us.

For now, those tales will serve as a framework for the telling of my own tale of my work with patients. Before going on to these tales, I would caution the reader by exposing yet another fairy tale, one in which every therapist believes from time to time.

Therapists know better than almost anyone else that all truth is subjective. They believe this to be the primary lesson they have to teach to patients. It is also the single most important and the hardest outlook for the therapist to sustain.

All therapists are vulnerable to mistaking their own world-view for reality. Ironically, we are perhaps even *more* vulnerable than most other people. The reason for this is as unfortunate as it is obvious. In all innocence, the fairy tale in which therapists most believe begins: "Once upon a time, there was a therapist who did not believe in fairy tales. . . ."

PART TWO

INNOCENCE AND EXPERIENCE

Little Lamb, who made thee?
Dost thou know who made thee?
. . . .
He is called by thy name,
For he calls himself a Lamb.
He is meek, & he is mild;
He became a little child.
William Blake, "The Lamb"

Tyger! Tyger! burning bright
In the forests of the night,
What immortal hand or eye
Could frame thy fearful symmetry?
. . . .
Did he smile his work to see?
Did he who made the Lamb make thee?
William Blake, "The Tyger"

5

If You Want to Know the Truth...

"If you want to know the truth. . . ." He must have said it at least a million times. For Holden Caulfield, this was both a catch-phrase and an incantation. He just couldn't stand imagining himself becoming a member of the phony world of grown-ups. He couldn't help it, for Chrissakes. Phoniness always drove him crazy, yet he had no goddam choice.

His hilarious and heartbreaking first-person account of that teenage struggle against the compromises of adulthood make up J. D. Salinger's novel *The Catcher in the Rye*.[1] Holden spoke for many kids of my generation. Thirty years and nine million copies later, his discontented vernacular continues to validate the feelings of successive generations of young people.

Holden would have been crazy about this success. Protecting childlike innocence and purity was what he wanted to do most in all the world. I remember when he tried to tell Old Phoebe about it. It was right after he flunked out of prep school. Not that he cared about that. It was so goddam phony he couldn't have stood it another minute without puking anyway.

He is unwilling to face his parents. Like most other grown-ups, they just didn't understand what's important. They were only interested in making money and in keeping up appearances. How can you ever expect to communicate with people like that? Holden has given up even trying anymore.

Instead he spends the week hiding out with other misfits in a seedy downtown hotel. He hangs out in crumby cocktail lounges trying unsuccessfully to make contact with other isolates. Depressed, having run out of money and patience, he decides to run away to the North Woods and farm the land. Pretending to be a deaf-mute so that no one will bother him, he may even end up marrying a genuine deaf-mute woman.

Slipping into his parents' apartment at night, he stops by to say goodbye to his kid sister, Old Phoebe. Before he leaves he shares with her his favorite fantasy of avoiding coming of age, his wish to become that Savior of Innocents, the Catcher in the Rye:

". . . I keep picturing all these little kids playing some game in this big field of rye and all. Thousands of little kids, and nobody's around—nobody big, I mean—except me. And I'm standing on the edge of some crazy cliff. What I have to do, I have to catch everybody if they start to go over the cliff—I mean, if they're running and they don't look where they're going. I have to come out from somewhere and *catch* them. That's all I'd do all day. I'd just be the catcher in the rye and all. I know it's crazy, but that's the only thing I'd really like to be." [2]

But Holden cannot save the children of this world. He cannot even save himself. Escape from the adult corruption of New York City did not take him to the pristine purity of the North Woods. *Catcher in the Rye* describes the threshold struggle of Holden as an idealistic East Coast sixteen-year-old. But the story is told in retrospect by the now seventeen-year-old patient of a California mental institution.

According to Holden, it was phoniness that finally drove him crazy. In the end it is not entirely clear to the reader whether the more destructive element was the phoniness of the grown-up world or his own. Some forms of madness are no more than failed transitions from one vision of life to the next.

Adolescence poses only one of the several natural developmental crises to be faced as we move on to each new phase of awareness. The turbulent awakenings that make up so much of the experience of being a teen-ager challenge our remaining innocence, demanding yet another complete transformation of our view of the world and of our own place in that world. The years of growth from mid-teens to young adulthood provide a time for the necessary transformation. This is the period during which our culture sanctions the individual's struggle against giving up an idealistic vision of the world as it should be for the disappointment of coming to terms with the world as it is.

This transformation from adolescent into young adult is foreshadowed by the evolvement from early childhood through puberty. Though both transitions involve monumental emotional changes and significant physical maturation, in the earlier of the two periods conceptual development is the central pivot. A large part of how a little kid becomes a big kid has to do with increasing a store of information and differentiating new ways of thinking.

The objectively curious child is learning how the physical/social world works. This understanding enables the child to predict and to control the environment more effectively. The subjectively self-conscious adolescent is reformulating value judgments about political, social, and personal relationships. This later reappraisal is demanded by growing awareness of the disparities between the ego ideal and the actual self, between the world as it should be and life as it is. Becoming a grown-up requires somehow fitting this imperfect person into a mismatched imperfect world.

The child needs to let go of a fairy-tale belief in how things work. The adolescent must abandon a romantically idealized vision of how things *should* work. Though at different levels, each must learn to make room for the role of chance.

The adolescent's emotional struggle against acceptance of the role of chance is foreshadowed in the younger child's uncomfortable intellectual encounter with the concept. Jean Piaget conducted experimental studies [3] of the origin of the idea of chance in youngsters ranging from preschoolers to twelve-year-olds.

Very young children retain a fairy-tale conceptual innocence about the workings of the physical world. They assume that there must be a good reason for anything that happens, and that in the end everything will turn out to be fair. It is not until shortly before puberty that they are able to make sense of the workings of a world so largely determined by chance happenings. In the interim between six and ten, when first they begin to lose this innocence, children are vulnerable to overwhelming hopelessness about the unmanageability of the universe. It is a time for learning concrete skills as a hedge against a life too random to be understood. Trying to figure it all out just seems too hard to handle.

This is an oversimplified picture of those years. Actually the losses of innocence come piecemeal, as does the temporary confu-

sion and eventual learning how to cope. Still, transitional periods
are difficult at any age. Biology offers a metaphor for the natural
vulnerability that comes with the transformations that occur each
time innocence is lost so that growth may occur.

In most insects the cuticle is so rigid that it must be discarded at in-
tervals to allow the animal to grow. This periodic shedding . . . is called
molting. The first step in molting is to produce a new cuticle under the
old one. This new cuticle is soft, white, and flexible and can be stretched.
Through pores in the new cuticle are poured enzymes that dissolve away
most of the old cuticle on the outside. By swallowing air or by . . . movements that squeeze blood into one part of the body, the insect bursts the
old cuticle. . . .

*Just after molting, the insect is vulnerable to predators, being unable
to move and lacking armor protection.* All in all, molting is one of the
most critical periods in the life of the insect, and the biology of this
event as it occurs in nature must be much more complex than is now
realized.[4]

The insect's molting offers a good metaphor for the human's
periodic shedding of protective shells of innocence. Without these
losses, there would be no possibility of increased awareness and expanded freedom. But each loss is accompanied by a period of vulnerability. Opportunities for further growth present themselves
again and again. Any particular loss of innocence may find us un-
ready to accept the helplessness required for the transformation.
For a time that particular opportunity must be set aside.

If it comes too early in life, the temporary vulnerability of transition will seem so unbearable that irreversible self-protective personality changes may result. In some instances readiness for change
may be further delayed by a person's having endured too many
painfully confusing experiences, or having received too little supportive care. In either case, the new vulnerability may be shielded
by a self-protective posture of pseudo-innocent denial.

Adolescence is not life's only period of transition. But it is during
this phase that personal growth is most obviously dependent on
the loss of innocence. It is also a time when people assume short-
lived dramatic postures to protect themselves from feeling overwhelmed during the transformation from childhood to adulthood.

To some extent, options for the sort of delaying posture an
adolescent assumes depend on the youth culture in which the teen-

age years are lived. The particular style of the adolescent's dramatic pose may be determined by that generation's subculturally sanctioned image. Over the past several decades we have seen the fashions change. The model of the twenties was the hedonist Flapper. From the thirties on we have seen the model shift from social-revolutionary young Marxists, to itinerant Beats, existential Hipsters, blissful pacifist Flower Children and yet-to-be-appraised teen-agers of the seventies. Individual family configurations and personality developments combine with class and regional differences to determine how the postures of particular teen-agers vary from the generally current style of his or her decade.

Whatever the changes, all adult communities complain about the antics of their young. Most provide begrudgingly sanctioned forms of rebellion.

The community sets up the options. The family can influence the length of time a young person is likely to be saddled with a particular brand of pseudo-innocence. Postures that begin as useful self-protection during the human molting period can become neurotic constraints beyond that time of transformation. The emotional hypocrisy of some family configurations encourage a teen-ager's dogged determination to cling to pseudo-innocence as a lifelong limitation. It is painful to see the phase-appropriate idealism or rebelliousness of adolescence overextended into a middle-aged mockery of itself.

Rigidly structured subcultures narrowly restrict their young people's options for creative protest against the adult hierarchy's idealizations of what life is all about. A teenager may be allowed isolated breaches of drunkenness and sulking, but politically effective organized group action such as barricading and boycotting would be unthinkable. The majority of young people growing up in stable, heavily tradition-bound communities are allowed to deviate only briefly and then in acceptably innocuous ways. Too soon they find that they have become the complacently oppressive, straight-arrow adults whose conventional wisdom they thought to challenge.

Emotional health is defined by such subcultures entirely in terms of adoption of communal standards. Unlike pluralistic societies, these bastions of tradition cannot tolerate the ambiguity that would result from allowing more than one form of acceptable behavior.

A surprisingly disproportionate number of delightful young people come to me for psychotherapy having made *un*satisfactory adaptations to rigidly structured subcultures. For example, many are the grown children of career foreign service and military families. They refer to themselves as "service brats" in a way that suggests that they view themselves as both a special breed and a particular bother.

In the tradition-bound setting in which they grew up, even very young children know just what is expected of them. Values are sloganized and behavior regulated by legalistic codes. (For example, it is not unusual for military families to post daily-duty rosters of the children's chores.)

Within these closed societies uniform values are everywhere in unmistakable evidence. Undergirded with patriotic slogans, elaborately structured hierarchies are elaborated by ideals of duty, responsibility, sacrifice, and a confusion of manners and morals.

Typically, father's career necessitated his repeatedly moving the family from one base to another, or absenting himself for months (or more) at a time during assignment to combat zones, naval cruises, or hazardous diplomatic posts. It is not unusual for a service brat to have lived in several countries and to have attended up to a dozen schools.

Imagine how painfully disruptive it must be for a youngster to be repeatedly uprooted each time he or she has just about got used to living in a particular town, finally made new friends, and learned to meet the expectations of an unfamiliar school system. Many times all of this must be managed with father far away and possibly in danger. Meanwhile, mother is expected to be the good soldier's wife, the officer's lady, or the associate diplomat. Her energy for the periodic chore of single-parenting is further divided by the social roles her husband's career demands of her. Within the limitations of this fragmented parenting, the service brat must adapt to multiple uprootings.

By the time service brats reach early adolescence, the whole charade has worn thin. No longer caught up in the ceremonially elaborated grown-up games of playing soldier, these kids begin to protest openly against the violations of their personal needs imposed by service life. The loss of innocent acceptance of communal values is at hand.

During this pivotal transition, configuration of the family plays a crucial role. If the parents genuinely believe in the service myths, the children of such straight-arrow families will make peace with the adult model of reality. Periodic relocating will be viewed as an advantage. The adolescent service brats will see themselves as more secure than their civilian counterparts who have been restricted to life in one town and attendance in a single school system.

Following the flag makes them feel at home anywhere in the world. Missing old friends and familiar places are considered shortsighted complaints about minor inconveniences that one gets used to. Not everyone gets to have a part in serving America and in defending the Free World. Living this dedicated mobile existence will some-day turn them into the sort of solidly reliable yet flexible people who can handle any damn thing that comes along.

The particulars of the pseudo-innocence foisted on service brats differ depending on whether they are boys or girls. The boys are asked to be good little soldiers. Their orders are to be brave, never to cry, and to take care of the fort till daddy comes home. Their enforced stoicism may give way to anger only if it is not mutinously directed against authority. It's okay to roughhouse, even to fight, and eventually to drink too much. As adolescents, their ways of blowing off steam will be begrudgingly tolerated if modeled after a new recruit's first three-day-pass spree. Eventually it is hoped that many will follow in the footsteps of father's military tradition.

Female service brats are expected to be comfortably composed, well mannered, and as little bother as possible. It is appreciated if they are neat and pretty. As adolescents they must be sophisticated in the social graces, appear chaste, and observe the military class distinctions (of enlisted personnel, noncommissioned and commissioned officers, line, field, and general grades of officers, etc.) Sanctioned adolescent protests for these girls are usually restricted to their insisting on going off to a boarding school rather than traveling with the family. One woman told me she thought foreign-service families were glad of this because by then these daughters were just "excess baggage." Curiously, though it is expected that they will someday marry, it is often hoped that they will make a good civilian match rather than continue in the male-sex-linked line of service families.

Ironically, those service brats who have grown up in neurotic family configurations have the best chance of becoming sufficiently misfit to enable their finding ways to escape into more individually defined ways of life. These kids responded to the emotional hypocrisy of their families with idiosyncratic pseudo-innocent postures of their own making. These compelling personal fantasies made them less likely to adapt successfully to the communal adult illusions to which "healthier" teen-agers succumb. Though each of these people came to me in the midst of great personal unhappiness, most showed remarkable creative potential that had survived despite their despair. It was as though their "neurotic" fantasies had protected them from sacrificing a personal inner fire for the paler glow of a more conforming merger with the community.

Here are two capsule examples of neurotic deviations from these service-brat patterns. In both cases seemingly maladaptive patterns protected the adolescent's valuable individual resources from being abandoned in the interest of more traditionally successful patterns of adjustment.

Some time ago a young man sought my help because he was chronically depressed, feeling that he was not worthwhile as a human being because he feared he might be homosexual. I was ready to help him either to dispel his fears that he was a homosexual or to find happiness with a fulfilled gay identity. As we explored his fears that he was not "a real man," his only solid evidence was a couple of authentically innocent moments of sexual tenderness with other young boys years before our meeting. His doubts had persisted because his own gently poetic nature did not measure up to his father's naval-officer man-at-the-mast macho toughness.

He was bright and self-disciplined enough to have been able to set aside his aesthetic inclinations in favor of entering the Naval Academy and emerging as a committed career officer. The family hypocrisy he had encountered deflected him from accepting the mastheads myths of manhood. Mother openly supported respect for father's real-man bravery under fire, while secretly taking on a draft-rejected artist as a lover.

It was clear to my patient that the commander knew himself to be a cuckold and deliberately denied this image-shattering defeat by concentrating attention on his naval victories. Unable to ally himself openly with either parent the kid imagined that he was "queer" and that they were not. In this way he could keep his world from coming apart by supporting it with the convenient fiction that if only he were not secretly homosexual he could be the man his father wanted him to be. At the same time he tried to channel his "latent femininity" into the poetic writings his mother so loved.

In the service-brat culture, he was categorized as a creep. The cost of this unacceptable self-portrait was chronic depression. Therapy allowed him to resolve that needless suffering while developing the poetic soul that had been spared by his not being able to live up to the demands of the community's standards.

Another service brat, this one a young woman, came to me for psychotherapy because of what she described as "a peculiar phobia about traveling." At first "peculiar" seemed like the right word for it. Unlike some other patients who fear traveling *alone*, this woman was afraid *only* when she went on a trip with a male friend.

As a political advocate of women's rights, she often traveled to strange cities on her own to attend, to appear before, or to run organizational conferences and workshops. In these roles she was tough, competent, and outspoken. Only on an out-of-town vacation weekend with a lover would she become panicky. Suddenly this strong, imaginatively independent woman became passive and clinging, "afraid I won't keep my mouth shut, that he'll get upset, hurt me and leave, and then I'll be lost and alone in a new place without any friends."

In exploring her service-brat upbringing, it became clear just how much pressure there had been on her to submerge her spirited independence in favor of being the colonel's uncomplainingly virginal daughter. It was the hypocrisy of the family myths that made the communal ideals unacceptable to her. On the surface, father seemed to soldier sincerely, while mother willingly wived. But the children grew up within the private horror of father's alcoholic abuse and mother's martyred whining. The children were forced to suffer along with her.

During adolescence, the emotional hypocrisy of the family made it impossible for her to accept the communal fairy tales. Unable to recognize mother's pseudo-innocent complicity in father's abusive treatment of the family, my patient was determined never to marry.

Instead she would devote her life to rescuing other brutalized women and children while playing out the role of the good parent she never had.

Her personal response to the family conflicts generated fantasy-laden behavior that quickly turned her into a social troublemaker within the Army Post community. It also perpetuated some needless private suffering, of which her travel phobia was but one small dramatic symptom. But out of all this also came a life of personally rewarding and politically significant work with the women's rights movement. She managed to transform her "troublemaking" into a creative capacity for social reform. *If you want to know the truth,* I believe that the personal pseudo-innocence of her neurotic style provided better raw materials for her eventual maturity than she ever would have found as a well-adjusted grown-up service brat.

My own history as a teen-age misfit was also that of a temporarily maladaptive, but eventually rewarding transformation. I remember my own adolescence as an unendingly painful and unhappy experience. Unaccountably, it just seemed to go on and on, well into my twenties. It was not that I experienced my adolescence as a fall from the grace and sweetness of childhood.

I fought a lot as a kid, not wisely and not well, but certainly often. Not thinking that I was worth much, I did not expect other children to like me. I sought attention on the streets as I had learned to get it at home—by making trouble. Even as a little kid, I didn't know how to make friends or how to join a group of other children at play. My style of social entry was to take their ball, to tease them, or to jump on some other kid's back. This usually resulted in my getting beaten up and then eventually being accepted, though as something of a scapegoat.[5]

Puberty seemed to offer new possibilities. For most of my life I did not understand that much of my needless social difficulty resulted from trying to live up to my parents' expectations. They saw me as a flawed extrovert, unpopular only because I "preferred being miserable." In truth I am a consummate introvert who was innocently trying to push against the grain of my natural temperament. I was destined to feel inadequate so long as I tried to be something other than myself.

By the time I reached puberty, I had just about given up. Unfortunately, my discovery that there was more to sex than masturbation motivated me for another doomed attempt to learn to get along with other people.

At the age of twelve or thirteen I found models for the sort of person I hoped to become. I was immediately drawn to two successfully extroverted schoolmates. For the next few years we were inseparable.

How I longed to learn to be able to please other people the way they did. Girls found them fun to be with. They were smooth talkers who could kid around without putting people off. I was sure that hanging around with these guys would allow me to learn to dance, to wear sharp clothes, and perhaps even to have lots of girls who let me feel them up. Getting into the crowd with Bobby and Jackie seemed to offer just the inspiration, tutoring, and encouragement I needed. Why they chose to spend time with me I could not understand. I accepted it as my first lucky break.

Of course, I remained myself. Hanging out with them helped some, but not much. I was the last one in the crowd to learn to dance, and my performance was always clumsy. I went to dances often, but usually hung around the bandstand pretending I had a sprained ankle. Under their extroverted guidance I bought sharp clothes. That didn't help either. Jackets never "hung right" on my klutzy shoulders.

I aspired to the macho four Fs of my generation: find 'em, feel 'em, fuck 'em, and forget 'em. Instead I was perpetually "in love," usually with someone unobtainable. When I did get close to a particular girl, we usually "went steady." In any case, it almost always turned out that she was "not that kind of girl."

Most of the guys in our crowd hoped someday to make it in show business. Some of them did. During our early teens they talked about their dreams of becoming musicians, actors, or stand-up comedians. I tried hard to smile at the running gag that I might become their business manager.

I thought my parents would be pleased to see me "put down the books already and go meet some people." Instead they criticized me for hanging around with "bums and loafers."

But these extroverted teen-agers did provide me a bridge to the world. We often went to Broadway vaudeville shows, following the Big Bands from one performance to another. Learning to smoke dope along the way, we ended up hanging around the jazz scene at the tiny clubs on 52nd Street. I was on my way to becoming streetwise. From Swing Street we went on to Harlem.

Soon my friends left. I stayed on for a while, mistakenly trying to find my Jewish self in a black experience. In my romanticized vision, only in black families could children and parents really communicate. And only as the single white person at an otherwise all-black party could I feel "at home." But in displacing my parents' Jewish fairy tale onto a racially integrated setting, I had simply assumed another pseudo-innocent posture. As I began to recognize its emptiness and hypocrisy, once more I experienced the painful isolation of the misfit.

Friendless and feeling like a fraud, I went back to hanging out in my old neighborhood. Ashamed of having no friends and "nothing to do on weekends," I half hoped that no one would notice my return. Unfortunately, for a while no one did. After a few months of wandering alone and lonely, I happened on a few other peculiar neighborhood late-teen-age isolates. They too seemed to live painfully unhappy, quietly misfit lives.

My neighborhood was composed mainly of families like my own. Most of the parents were the children of Jewish Eastern European immigrants. Only partially assimilated themselves, they were ashamed of the foreign origins of their parents. They struggled to be successful Americans, but it was often not exactly clear to them just what one had to do to become fully a "Yankee."

For the many teen-age Jewish boys in the neighborhood there were two acceptable roles. Being a good student was the preferred posture, leading as it did to someday becoming "a professional man." However, allowances were made for those boys who did not do well in school, if they were well mannered or athletic instead. They too could someday become completely respectable members of the adult community, provided that they stayed out of trouble, married nice neighborhood girls, and went into their fathers' businesses.

The misfits that drifted together and made my own life bearable at that stage fitted neither mold. There were a half-dozen of us who were probably the brightest and the worst kids in the neighborhood. All of us were "emotionally disturbed." None of us had learned (or was willing) to use creative intelligence to get the good grades that would have pleased our parents. Our aggressiveness was too subversive to serve for athletic competition.

Somehow we found one another. It wasn't so much that we liked each other. It was more a matter of desperately needing the company of other misfits. Together we drifted down to Greenwich Village. As a band of young misfits, we fit there. Defining ourselves as "The Neo-Nihilists," we did what we could to get thrown out of one espresso coffeehouse after another. We greeted passersby with a loud "Hi Digger," threw books at intellectuals, and accused folksingers of not being real folks. It was all harmless enough, but I would have hated knowing it at the time.

One evening two or three of us entered a crowded Village bar. It was difficult to get the bartender's attention. There were many other customers. Besides, none of us knew how to handle even as simple a social situation as that one. I was to order beers for the three of us. At last a kindly looking middle-aged Irish bartender acknowledged my awkward attempts to get served.

In a voice that seemed awfully loud even in that crowded din, he shouted, "What'll it be, Moishe?" Competent enough at least to get a beer at a bar, I had experienced the momentary satisfaction of being in command. The feeling was quickly shattered. The bartender was smiling in a friendly enough way, but the remark sounded clearly anti-Semitic. "Moishe" is a Jewish name for Murray, often used as an ethnic stereotype equivalent to the name "George" or "Rastus" for a black. I was bewildered. I was also outraged. "Moishe!" I shouted back. "What the hell is the idea of calling me 'Moishe'? I don't know you and that's not my name. What the hell are you trying to tell me?"

The bartender leaned forward, softening his posture so that I would understand he was not about to attack me. Though he continued to speak loudly enough for me to hear over the noise of the crowd, his tone was gentle and intimate. "I didn't mean to offend you, kid," he soothed. "Don't you know what a 'Moishe' is? A 'Moishe' is a bright Jewish kid from Brooklyn or the Bronx who doesn't get along well enough with his parents to be willing to study hard at school. If you throw him a ball he puts out his hands. The ball goes right between them and hits him in the head. After a while he gets unhappy with his neighborhood and ends up hanging out down here in the Village for a while." I had been given a sanctioned identity. At last, I fit in. Gratefully I over-tipped the bartender for his beer and sympathy.

We were all "Moishes." One of us was a talented young painter who eventually became so obsessively immersed in the philosophical exploration of the religio-aesthetic implications of being an artist that he gave up painting. Last I heard he was in his thirties, out of work, and back in the Bronx living with a mother he could not stand.

Another had once aspired to become a scientist. I remember his bitter complaint that he had been tricked by junior high school teachers into believing in an unreal version of the universe. In high school he was taught that that was not quite the way it was. The new cosmology he learned in high school was once again discredited in college science courses. Science turned out to be no more reliable than his family's fairy tale that if only he studied hard and behaved himself, he would no longer feel confused and unhappy.

That was too much to take. He dropped out of school averring that someday the science teachers would discover that $2 + 2 = 5$, and then all over the world the machines would stop running and the lights would go out. Still fascinated by chemistry he turned to heroin to ease the pain of his recurrent losses of innocence. Before he reached thirty, he died of an overdose.

Another soulful savior in our crowd ended up as a Village bartender trying to rescue other misfits. A few years age he came to visit me in Washington. He explained that it had been a dull week in New York so he decided that he ought to go to Boston or Washington or somewhere for the weekend.

Remembering having heard that I had long ago moved to Washington, he decided to look me up. By then he had become unofficial mayor of the Village, full of wonderfully colorful stories and hoping someday to "get somewhere." He was in his forties and some months earlier had moved in with yet another twenty-year-old girl. If the relationship lasted another year he thought he would marry this one and settle down. Without either of us saying so, we both knew that when she reached twenty-one, he would split and move in with some other twenty-year-old.

Like myself, the brightest member of our crowd had chosen to pursue a career as a psychotherapist. Last heard of, after a dozen years he was working in a hopelessly monolithic mental institution and suing Yeshiva University for his still unawarded Ph.D.

I separated from these other life-saving misfits when it turned out that I was the only one to pass the preinduction psychiatric examination during the Korean War. Up to that point we had each done what we could to delay being drafted. I was the only one too rigidly righteous to carry on at the induction center. One of us was rejected for lisping through lipstick put on for the occasion. Another avoided military service by answering the doctor's question "How do you get along with people?" by asking in turn, "Do you mean Earth people?" Still another went for his examination so strung out on drugs that they kept him overnight before sending him home as a 4-F. The rest would not even tell me how they had managed to "fool the shrink."

Those were proud and painful times. I'm glad they're over. Still, sometimes I miss them. In retrospect, the exaggerated poses I struck during those transitional years often seem funny. Sometimes they seem pathetic. No matter. They served me well through that painful transformation from child to adult.

Some youthful defiance turns out to be no more than momentary immersion in a socially sanctioned form of protest. Most young people seem to participate in communally fashioned fads, striking postures determined more by peer-group pressure than by the individualized shaping of their own inner needs. The assurance of having been members of the majority within the adolescent subculture becomes their preparation for a future of unexamined complacency as Establishment adults.

I am grateful that my own molting was more marginal. By consciously surrendering to being the misfit I was, I realize I risked further isolation. Perhaps that is the price of insisting on living life in your own way. But not even the willingness to pay that price guarantees a happy adult life later on. Though less likely to lead to complacency, the more individualized adolescent paths may also end up in the wilderness. The eventual adult lifestyles of misfit adolescents is harder to predict than those of kids whose teen-age postures were more communally determined. Young misfits seem to end up in a wider spectrum of adult roles ranging from Christs to crackpots.

Positions forged in the heat of youthful passion may later be tempered into resiliently lasting creative efforts. Though originating as a hedge against adolescent vulnerability, individually determined attitudes can develop into an integrated sense of self in adulthood.

Everyone goes through the adolescent crisis of discovering that life is not at all what we as children had been led to believe it was. Suddenly nothing makes sense anymore. This confrontation with the discrediting of the original fairy tales is too overwhelming to be taken in all at once. Momentarily stripped of innocence we stand nakedly vulnerable to the rawness of a life without meaning. Each of us must find a way to put off the seemingly unbearable prospect of becoming a grown-up. Some cling to the hope of reestablishing an idealized image of the world. Others set out to become the person one *should be* in quixotic struggle with the world *as it is*. In either case, temporarily life must be simplified. Contradictions in the self and ambiguities in the world must be obscured by the illusion that life is meaningful, understandable, and finally manageable. As Camus points out: "A world that can be explained even with bad reasons is a familiar world." [6] Small children insist on hearing the same fairy tales again and again. The adults who read them aloud dare not change a word.

Each of us had to find some way to delay our awakening. This pseudo-innocent hedge is no more than a natural phase of adolescence, though for some this phase may last a lifetime.

6

Momma's Boy and Daddy's Little Girl

Pampering a child may also contribute to delaying the loss of innocence necessary to the eventual development of a more grown-up vision of his or her place in the world. Sons raised as momma's boy and daughters as daddy's little girl often grow up burdened with an exaggerated sense of self-importance and handicapped by a particularly naïve sense of what will bring them happiness. The doting opposite-sex parents of these young favorites encourage life-long expectations of being the center of special attention. So often praised and given their own way, pampered children grow up with an apparent air of self-confidence.

On the surface, this seems like a favorable setting in which to be raised. More careful inspection reveals that often such children are used and misled in ways that may cost them needless suffering as adults.

The seductive situation of seeming to be favored not only over siblings but even over the parent of the same sex is a heady fantasy image for the kid. But it can get pretty confusing in such a father/daughter relationship when daddy abandons his little princess to go off for a two-week vacation alone with his otherwise scorned wife. It sometimes takes a lifetime for such people to accept the simple fact that momma and daddy had chosen each other before the child was born and that they choose to go on together after the child has grown up and left home. The favored child has been given a grossly exaggerated sense of his or her own importance. In their innocence it comes as a shock to learn that home life goes on in their absence, that the family of origin is a temporary scene in which the child is only passing through. Such people are ill-prepared for the world's indifference.

Momma's adulation for her wonderful little boy may turn out to be little more than a continuing reminder to her husband that she is not satisfied with their marriage. The favored child who is used as a means of criticizing and controlling a mate learns to share the doting parent's contempt for the same-sex parent.

Only the favoring parent's approval is worth seeking. This makes the child a set-up for yet another kind of exploitation as a sort of second chance for the doting parent to realize his or her own missed opportunities. The child is used as a screen on which the favoring parent can watch projections of unlived self-expectations. Sometimes favored children become singularly accomplished adults, but many someday wake up wondering why they've chosen a way of life that does not suit them.

Beneath a seemingly smug attitude of apparent self-confidence lies doubt about whether they are worth anything at all. This seeming belief in their own abilities is a thin and brittle veneer. The favored child grows up expecting to go on getting away with avoiding the disappointments and frustrations that others have learned must be faced. Doting parents "spoil" their favorite children. It is not a matter of the child being given too much. It is only that often the parent does not insist on giving what the child needs. Instead the child is given either what the parent wanted but had to do without or, worse yet, is regularly given his or her own way. This kind of parental indulgence makes the child feel adored by and adoring of the parent but it is poor preparation for later living unprotected in a world that grants no special favors for simply being well behaved or adorable.

Bright and able as some of these pampered children may be, unreadiness for dealing with a world in which they are not favored often makes them seem like foolish adults. They may be clearly accomplished and sensitive in many ways, but again and again they will seem incredibly naïve. Their seemingly innocent expectations of certain success are an ineffectual denial that they are no longer special. Even when they realize that their efforts are senseless, their response is more likely to be tantrum than surrender to life as it is.

Often this irrationally self-destructive behavior is no more than the stubborn insistence that no one will be able to resist giving in to their manipulations. Having had their whims so long indulged as though they were little princes or princesses makes the ordinary life of a commoner inevitably disappointing.

When such people act dumb as grown-ups it is usually out of a willful insistence that the whole world treat them as their parents did. This senseless form of pseudo-innocence is demonstrated clearly in Flaubert's classic novel *Madame Bovary*.[1] "It is no exaggeration to say that the whole novel grows out of this. . . . Stupidity is the major theme and Romantic illusion simply one of its forms."[2]

Within this limited focus on that complex novel I will concentrate my attention. The more lasting literary and sociological, and the more broadly psychological, implications of this book have been carefully considered by many others. Flaubert is generally regarded as the father of realism, creator of the contemporary novel, and pivotal critic of romanticism. Stylistically he managed to suggest the feelings of his characters without direct description or analysis. He was able to depict their psychological characters within a socio-logical context that portrayed his disdain for the hollowness of nine-teenth-century bourgeois culture. Even so, Flaubert's criticism of self-deception was tempered with compassion. Sympathetically he understood that we all fool ourselves at times.

On the surface the Bovary story is an account of the unhappy marriage of an unfulfilled, longingly romantic young woman and a complacently dull country doctor. In desperation, Emma takes lovers who inevitably desert her. She is reduced to settling for the material trappings of her dreams of romantic elegance by purchas-ing the luxuries that will make her feel special. She hides her extrav-agance from Charles (as he hides it from himself). Inevitably they fall hopelessly into debt. Faced with the exposure of her sexual and fiscal infidelities, Emma commits suicide. Charles, in turn, dies of a broken dream.[3]

Examined more closely, much of their suffering seems needless. Both have been trapped within their own illusions. Each clings to a vision of life as it should be rather than as it is. As a result they miss any of the opportunities for happiness offered by their actual life together.

From a sociological perspective, Charles's and Emma's dangerous illusions may be respectively interpreted as representing bourgeois complacency and romantic escapism. Psychologically they may be understood as those forms of pseudo-innocence that are imposed on the pampered child.

Charles Bovary was a momma's boy. For years, his mother had suffered disregard and humiliation at the hands of her self-centered, flamboyantly unfaithful husband. In her unhappiness she shifted all of her attention to the possessively domineering pampering of her son. Momma spoiled and babied Charles while shaping his life toward becoming the sort of man/child who she hoped could make her happy. She hadn't counted on turning him over to the likes of Emma.

Emma just misses being the classical daddy's little girl. She was not so much her widowed father's little darling as the decorative object of his good-natured, sentimental devotion to easy living. He spoiled her by indulging her whims, and provided her with education and dreams that her social position would never allow her to fulfill. But once she was married off, he readily redirected his energies to his own self-indulgence.

Charles's domineering mothering turned him into a passive man devoted to pleasing women. Once married, he continued to expect that everyone would be happy if only he was well behaved. His trained attention to appearances left him empty of sensitivity to inner emotions. Looking around and seeing that he had become a doctor who provided his wife with a well-furnished house, pretty clothes, and a comfortable life, he could not believe that she might be unhappy. Possession of a lovely wife whom he was always ready to please was enough to maintain his respect for himself. He was sure Emma would be happy to be married to such a good boy.

But Emma found Charles's company

. . . as flat as a street pavement, on which everybody's ideas trudged past, in their workaday dress, provoking no emotion, no laughter, no dreams. . . . His ardours had lapsed into a routine, his embraces kept fixed hours; it was just one more habit, a sort of dessert he looked forward to after the monotony of dinner.[4]

She dreamed of the elegance of Paris theaters and palace balls that would make her feel like the princess she longed to be.

When Emma finally did act out her romantic longings, the

yearned-for bliss, passion, and ecstasy of which till now she had only read were not the result of being loved by a man who treated her better than Charles did. Instead they came from an enhanced fairy-tale vision of herself reflected in a bedroom mirror.

Never had her eyes looked so big, so dark, so deep; her whole person had undergone some subtle transfiguration. "I've a lover, a lover," she said to herself again and again. . . .[5]

Believing that his passive obedience to a woman would make her happy, Charles ignored the obvious expressions of Emma's discontent. Certain that, for her, happiness could come only from being specially adored, Emma "rejected as useless whatever did not minister to heart's immediate fulfillment." [6] Emma could not bear having to ask Charles for what she wanted. If he *really* loved her, he would have known without having to be told. She blinded herself to the obvious dangers that her recklessly romantic adventures would surely bring to pass. With simple fairy-tale innocence, Emma insisted that "since life had not been kind to her so far, the future must surely hold something better in store for her." [7]

Pampered children are raised to expect that they will always be treated as little princes and princesses. Again and again they have been told, "No matter how big you get, you'll always be daddy's little girl (or momma's darling baby boy)." This message would impose no special burden if eventually it could be clearly understood to mean no more than "You will always be important to me because I so enjoy the special feeling of being the loving parent." Instead it is heard in a context that invites the belief that it is the child who possesses some special charm that will always enchant other people.

I knew one woman who was convinced that "Every man I meet falls at least a little bit in love with me." Much of her energy was invested in being seductive. Most men's impersonal sexual responses were mistaken for love. This "adoration" was taken for granted by this woman and met with disdain. Obvious disinterest from any particular man was experienced by her as a bewildering rejection. Her neurotic lifestyle was centered on pursuit of such detached men. Not getting her way with them left her depressed and self-critical. When she was able to engage such a man, a brief, intense affair would ensue but soon she would lose interest. Afterward the only attachment that remained was the desperate wish that the discarded suitor would go on loving and missing her for the rest of his unhappy life.

Once at a dinner party I met a middle-aged man who had obviously not yet gotten over having been raised as a little prince. When we all sat down at the dinner table, his face lit up with a smile of great self-satisfaction. At first I mistook this smile to be an indication of how much he enjoyed eating; suddenly, without warning, his overly loud voice demanded all of our attention to the gratuitous announcement: "You know, I've always been a good eater." Forty-five years old and he expected the rest of us to admire him as his momma must have when he ate all his oatmeal.

My own childhood involved a good deal of maternal pampering. I too could have grown up believing that others would treat me as though I were a little prince. But I was saved from the unhappy ending of one fairy tale by the ominous beginnings of another. Though ready to play queen mother to her special baby boy, my momma was disconcerted by her belief that I was a *changeling*.

Parents have long been protected from having to accept responsibility for children who reveal traits that the parents find unacceptable in themselves. Much is made of these awful characteristics when first they are discovered in (or projected onto) the newborn baby.

The traditional belief in changelings concerned one child being substituted or changed for another. In the Scottish highlands, babies were strictly watched over before their christenings. Until then an infant might be stolen from its cradle by fairies. In its place they would leave an unsatisfactory substitute. Any ugly, weakly, or peevish child was likely to be considered a changeling. This allowed the good mother to raise a discredited imperfect child without being blamed for its faults.

More contemporary disowning is usually stated in terms of projected blaming of absent relatives: "Listen to that baby holler. She has grandma's temper." Or, "Only two weeks old and he's too lazy to drink his milk. Another Uncle Harry . . . he won't accomplish anything either."

My own mother's outlook was more traditional and her condemnation more comprehensive. Over and over she told me that there *must* have been a mix-up at the hospital. Surely some other lucky mother must have taken home the good baby with which she should have been blessed.

Now she was stuck with the wrong child. "I love you, but I don't like you," she would tell me. Even though I was an undesirable changeling, she would try to raise her little frog as though he were a prince.

And so, though reminded daily that I was a bad child, I was also given the royal treatment accorded a son in a typical Jewish-American child-centered home.[8] I was pampered, indulged, overprotected, and made the almost constant center of the family's attention. Again and again I was told that if I really cared, then all of these advantages would enable me to become the wonderful achieving son I was meant to be.

Perhaps the clearest single example of pampering was the way in which my mother started me out each day going off to grade school. She and my father and I lived in a small apartment in a six-story walk-up in the Bronx. Limited family income restricted us to renting a top-floor apartment. Living in these low-cost flats meant climbing long flights of stairs each day, and being among the last tenants to have their radiators hot on cold winter mornings.

On weekdays during those chilling months my mother would get up at dawn when it was "so cold only a mother could stand it." Selecting freshly laundered underwear and socks from my dresser drawer, she would place them on the radiator to warm. I would not be awakened until she could announce, "Now you can get up. You shouldn't have to worry because your mother has already been up in the freezing apartment heating clothes to warm her *nisht-guteh's* (no good one's) tootsies and his sweet little *toosh*." She would lift a corner of my bedcover just enough to hand me warmed socks, underwear, and my morning dose of guilt.

Within the limits that my parents could financially afford (and sometimes beyond them), I was given the best of everything. My mother told me she wanted me to taste the good things in life, to learn to feel that I could not do without them. This would later motivate me to go after everything I wanted aggressively. Then I would surely become a success, a big professional man, if only I did not end up in prison and break a mother's heart.

My mother was always ready to extend to me the privileges demanded by my station of princeling. But like her pampering, the special protection she offered was shaped by her recognition of my changeling wildness. As an infant I was wrapped in swaddling. She later told me that whenever I was unwrapped, I would get so excited that I had to be rebound quickly so that I would not hurt myself with all of my flailing about.

My mother's loving constraints were aimed at protecting me from my own destructive nature. During my first experience as a psychotherapy patient some of the residue of this protection surfaced dramatically. My young Freudian therapist believed that the solving of neurotic problems depended on the patient's telling his or her story in order to find out how it began. He encouraged me to devote much of my attention to the discovery and exploration of my earliest memories.

I would have done almost anything to please him. He seemed like an older brother who might once have been as stuck emotionally as I and who had learned to break free. Following his lead, I too would be able to get out on my own. As instructed, I spent many hours trying to come up with my very earliest memory.

My most long-ago image turned out to be a dim recollection of having been trapped within a circle of women. Symbolically, it fit the consciously conflicted love-hate relationships with women that had first brought me to seek therapy. Therapy had helped me to understand one of my central conflicts. I longed to be cared for and held by a good mother. At the same time, rebelling against my own mother's domineering attitudes, I fearfully fought off the very closeness I was seeking.

Obsessively I examined the relation of this image to my projected fears that women wanted to control me. Analyze as we might, both the therapist and I ended up feeling that there was something of substance that we missed understanding in all of this. He explained to me that obviously the image of the circle of women was a *screen* memory. This fantasied happening served my psychic economy by masking some more upsetting *actual* happening in my early childhood. Once we were able to interpret correctly my associations to this fantasy image, memory of the actual earlier experience would become conscious, and the trauma would set me free.

At the time, both my therapist and I were somewhat overintellectualized in our approaches to problem-solving. Stubbornly insisting that the unexamined life was not worth living, we were inclined to ignore the reciprocal truth: that the unlived life is not worth examining. Certain that our devotion to conjecture would yield the truth, we wasted a good deal of our time and energy (and my money) in hypothesizing.

Out of desperation, and in rebellion against what I began to experience as authoritarian psychoanalytic dogma, I decided on a drastic course of action. Instead of restricting my research to free association, dreams, and fantasies, it finally occurred to me that I might simply go home and ask my mother about my childhood. Her accounts of early trauma might help me to understand this fragmented screen memory of imagining that I had been trapped within a circle of women.

My mother was delighted to be of help. She knew exactly what it was that I must have been remembering. Excitedly she told me: "Even from the time you were a little baby, you were like some wild animal. That's why I got grandma to show me how to wrap you. The moment you were too old to be wrapped, you began getting into all the trouble you could. You never learned to walk. You only learned to run. And whenever you ran, you fell down and upset me. Even a little boy, if he was the right sort of child, could care about a mother not to get himself hurt as often as you did.

"I had to take you downstairs to the street so that you could have the fresh air and sunshine a little boy needs. But I knew that if I didn't keep you under control you would get yourself killed. What did you care? Such a wild one! There was only one way to handle a boy like you.

"So I used to get all the other mothers to help. They at least had children you didn't have to watch every minute. So I would get all these mothers to sit around with me in a circle. We sat on milk crates from the grocery. And then you could play safely in the circle where I wouldn't have to worry what you might do next.

"Of course, you only wanted to break out of the circle so that you could get hurt. But a mother loves her child, wild as he is, and so we always kept you inside the circle. The other mothers would ask: 'Where did you get such a wild one?' And I would always tell them: 'Where did I get him? That same place you got yours, from the hospital. Only they gave me the wrong one, so he needs a little special attention.'

"The circle of women that you remember is the embrace of a loving mother protecting her bad boy."

My mother's preoccupation with my well-being ranged from these destructive constraints to genuinely caring protectiveness. One instance involved some question of my suffering from rickets. I will never be certain whether or not there was any medical basis for my never learning to walk "like a human being." According to my family, as soon as I could walk, I ran. Often when I ran, I fell down.

Having raised three active sons of my own, that sounds to me no different from the normal behavior of most little kids. It is a developmental phase that usually provokes some manageable parental anxiety. But for my mother it had been a frantic time. She was sure that I would get myself killed. Something had to be done about my wildness. Because I had outgrown the age of swaddling, I was next offered the protective constraints of the magic circle of mothers. For many years skates, bicycles, and other mother-threatening demonic devices were strictly forbidden.

When it was suggested that my "walking problem" might have some underlying medical cause, my mother took me from one doctor to another. If there was something really wrong with me, she wanted it cured. It was all very confusing to me. On the one hand, I could feel that she really wanted to save me from being hurt. But when I did fall down, she was likely to remind me with "See how God punishes a child who doesn't listen to his mother."

My mother's craziness made some of her pampering and protectiveness grotesque and destructive. Even so, I am left with a strong sense of having been a favored child guarded by a strong, caring mother. This feeling is immediately evoked by one story, told and retold over the years.

Once my parents became convinced that there might be something physically wrong with me, there was no stinting on investing the family's limited finances and my mother's boundless energies in finding a cure for their ailing son. I was taken to "the biggest men" among the expensive Park Avenue doctors, the New York Jewish equivalent of Lourdes.

I was still a preschooler when we visited the "top" orthopedic specialist. My mother told me the story many times. This is her account of his examination, diagnosis, and recommendation, and of her own rendering of the final expert second opinion: "I told him about your problem. He had me take off your pants so that he could examine you himself. He took one look and told me 'Malformed bones. We'll have to break both his legs and put them in casts.' Your mother gave one listen and told him, 'Break your head and put it in the garbage.' "

Out of her own madness, she hurt me most when she was trying to protect me from my own "wildness." But she never let anyone else hurt me. My childhood was bad and it was good.

My parents delivered mixed messages about the ways that I was special to them. Most of the time I felt confused by their peculiar combination of dutiful indulgence and punitive restriction. They gave and gave and gave to me, but most often they gave what they needed to give rather than what I needed to receive. Even when their generosity met my needs, there was usually a quality of undoing about the offerings.

As I was entering puberty, just so that I could have a room of my own, we moved to a larger, more expensive apartment. They could ill afford the rent increase. But "a boy needs a room, so a boy gets a room." I was deeply appreciative and very excited. It meant that my growing up was being respectfully acknowledged. They were making space for my having a place of my own in which to develop beyond the role of the family's little boy. I told them how grateful I was to be given a room that would allow that privacy and independence.

Additionally, I was secretly delighted imagining having a room of my own that would give me greater freedom to masturbate. I made the mistake of asking if I might install some simple lock on the *inside* of the door of my room. Confronting the problem squarely, my mother replied, "How will a mother get in to clean her son's room?"

I pointed out that obviously the room would only be locked at times when I was inside. When I was out, she could come and go as she pleased. If she found the door locked, she need only knock, and I could let her in. She explained to me that this was a bad idea because then she would have to interrupt me when I was doing my homework. If my studies were disturbed, how would I ever get to become a doctor?

From her point of view, there was nothing more to be discussed. There would be no lock. To lend an air of authority to her tentative suggestions, she summoned my father from the newspaper-reading living-room chair that served as his den. "Sidney, get in here," she commanded. "It's time for you to get your ungrateful son to show some respect for you." My father came in *slowly*. It was his only way of demonstrating that no one could push him around.

"Now tell him," she ordered. "Tell your son that he's a big boy now. We have given him his very own room. Who will clean up the mess? Only his mother, who else? So now tell him that he must be grown-up enough to let his mother come into his very own room whenever she wants."

My father's silent compliance was always maintained with the simple dignity of a man whose mere presence lent authority to this woman's foolish whims. Assured by his wordless sanction, my mother went on: "A lock yet he wants. A lock he won't get. You heard what your father said. So that's that! A boy doesn't argue with a father."

Decorating was another problem that came with being grown-up enough to have my own room. I was a very special boy whose parents would see to it that he had a brilliant future. Such a boy does not have a room decorated with pennants and posters. My most treasured trophy, a swiped traffic sign, was not even permitted into the house.

Like the rest of the apartment, my room was to be redecorated annually. Ceremonially, my mother would announce, "It's time for you to decide how you would like your very own room to look this year. The best stores are all showing sailing themes for a boy's room. Yesterday I already saw a beautiful ship's lantern you'll use as a bed lamp, little anchors for clothing hooks, and a gorgeous big sailing chart for the wall above your desk. You don't have to worry about it. It's all picked out. You'll love it. Nothing but the best. When you're a famous doctor, you'll have a sailboat all your own. Who knows? If you'll be a surgeon, your mother will someday get to go for a cruise on her son's very own yacht."

No matter what the chosen annual redecoration motif, one perennial piece of decor remained, a symbol of the constraints on any attempt to outgrow being my momma's boy. Whatever the new decorative theme, there remained a permanent corner shelf on which my bronzed baby shoes were enshrined. In fairness, I would like to point out that among people of my parents' generation, it was not unusual to bronze such keepsakes. But mine is the only home I know of that displayed them in the room of the embarrassed teen-ager who had once worn them.

With no lock on the door to stop her, it was not unusual for my mother to enter my room unannounced, leading an entourage of visiting Mah-Jongg players. She would show off her very own son to these women, just as she showed off how beautifully I had decorated my very own room.

My bronzed baby shoes were the highlight of the tour. After allowing time for the spontaneous oohing and ahing of the other Mah-Jongg mothers, she would display the ultimate poignancy. Adoringly, my mother would lift the tiny shoes down from the shelf on which they were enshrined. Pointing out the eternalized bronzed wrinkles in what had once been baby-soft white leather, she would remind us all of the trickles of urine that they memorialized. "Can you imagine?" she would sigh. "This boy who is studying so that some day he will go to college, and then on to medical school, this big horse who is almost a doctor was once a cute little *pisher*. Big as he is, to me he'll always be momma's little boy."

All through my puberty and early adolescence I argued petulantly against her keeping those shoes in my room. For a while those futile arguments were the only evidence that natural growth forces remained intact within me. I was sixteen before I got around to dumping those humiliating bronzed treasures in a faraway garbage can. For years I believed that getting my mother to see it my way was my only hope. It took an awfully long time before I realized that whether or not she understood, I still could do as I pleased. That painful delay is a tribute to the seductive power of being cast as momma's boy.

The feeling of being someone special is almost hypnotically compelling. Entranced by that naïve belief, momma's boy and daddy's little girl expect to be recognized as marvelous creatures wherever they go. It is bewildering when one day such a person discovers that he or she was grown up to be an unremarkable adult surrounded by unimpressed strangers.

No longer singled out for special attention, admiration, and pampering, the once favored child must somehow come to terms with living in a world that hardly recognizes his or her existence. Such a person may go on pretending to be the chosen one by selectively ignoring or explaining away the experiences of being treated with indifference.

The personal and social costs can be very high for those who persist in the fantasy of being the favorite child. Over-aged versions of momma's boy and daddy's little girl may be seen by others as conceited, aloof, or simply as unreasonably demanding. Paradoxically, as a result they may be less sought after than other people. Unwilling to settle for being liked by some but not by others, the person who insists on being favored by everyone may end up being liked by no one.

At those times, when the vision of being special is effectively threatened by other people's reactions, it is as though everything has been ruined. Life may become a roller-coaster ride of exorbitantly excited fantasy expectations inevitably followed by unbearably disappointing experiences. When they are simply being treated like everyone else, momma's boy and daddy's little girl feel rejected. We all dislike not getting our own way. Life is filled with simple frustrations that most people can meet with mild disappointment, resignation, and hope for the future. At such times momma's boy and daddy's little girl invariably feel "hurt." They demand vengeance or compensation. This petulance almost guarantees repetition of their needless disappointments.

During one of these painful lows, such people sometimes seek the help of a psychotherapist. Early in my work I accepted several of them into individual psychotherapy. Some would be reassuringly nourished by their experience of receiving that special attention. Soon they would be hopeful once more that the world would adore them just as momma or daddy had. Almost invariably they would leave therapy at that point for another turn on the roller-coaster ride that had become their life.

Later in my career, I decided to offer group-therapy experience to such patients. Some refused, insisting that they had special problems requiring individual attention. For those who did enter a group, the therapeutic value seemed to me to be something of a resocialization process. During months of interaction and exploration these "favorites" learned greater awareness and more tolerance for the frustrations of living in the world as ordinary people. It was difficult to keep them from being scapegoated by the group. When I failed to interrupt that furor effectively, they left too early for their own good. The other members were usually delighted, seeing their leaving as little more than a temper tantrum.

Now that I have become clearer about the kind of therapy I wish to do, I no longer conduct groups. I view my first meeting with any prospective individual therapy patient as our getting together to see if we like each other well enough to spend that much time alone with each other. Treating myself well in this way is one of the creative outgrowths of having once been pampered.

There are also some less attractive residuals of the pampered child about me. My wife and I and our sons join another family for an evening cookout on the beach. It is just this side of sunset. Without hesitation, everyone else (including the kids) sets to gathering firewood, digging a barbecue pit, spreading the blankets, and unpacking the food. I discover that everyone else has readily recognized what needed to be done and has begun doing it. Once again I find that only I am sitting watching the sun set and waiting to be served my din-din.

Such discoveries used to evoke a deep sense of shame in me. To ameliorate my distress I would sometimes pester the others for reassurance. "You must understand that I have the soul of an artist." "You must forgive me for my 'compulsive' laziness." These days I play the pampered child less often. And should I catch myself doing so, I'm usually not ashamed anymore. I may be mildly embarrassed and uncomfortably amused by my antics, but I'm not willing to go on investing them with the attention required to maintain shame. Without comment, I set about doing my part of the work to which we are all committed. None of us is special. Together we create the setting for what usually turns out to be an evening enjoyed by all.

Because of my own need to feel special, I am sometimes impatient with like attitudes in people who come to me for psychotherapy. Recently an attractive, well-spoken professional woman began an initial interview with the mild complaint that she was "too controlling" and wanted to improve herself in that regard. She seemed to have no doubt that I would be happy to spend time with her.

Unsolicited, she offered me a glowing appraisal of her upbringing. It had been the most wonderful of childhoods. Oh, mother could sometimes be a bit of a pest, but daddy was always marvelous. She had been his favorite in all the world. In fact, she still was, and always would be. She adored daddy. He treated her as his little princess. He would do just anything to make her happy.

All during this account, her previously soft throaty voice tone took on the strained, deliberately bright quality of an amateur actress broadcasting her first laundry-detergent commercial. It seemed to me that she had successfully learned to mask some terrible secret pain. Hidden desperation had narrowed the focus of her considerable imagination in the service of projecting a reassuringly oversimplified, too-good-to-be-true advertising image. She dismissed my suggestion that she needed to hide how bad she really felt.

Along the way she inserted a parenthetic-sounding running commentary on what she was saying. This distracting alternate monologue qualified the pseudo-innocent childlike excitement with psychologically sophisticated asides such as, "Of course, I realize that this is an idealization," "We had all the normal developmental parent-child struggles," and the like.

When I suggested that it must be a burden to have to monitor her thoughts that way, she protested that this "insightfulness" was one of the many traits that delighted her. She had no more wish to change it than to give up feeling like a princess. With the exception perhaps of her being a bit too controlling of others, there was little that she wanted changed in her already wonderful life. She seemed totally unaware of the smugness communicated by her almost flawless air of self-satisfaction.

Put off by how self-controlled and aloof she seemed, I told her that I wasn't at all sure I wanted to work with someone who showed so little vulnerability.

Learning that she had not impressed me seemed to bewilder her. I was unprepared for the transformation. The seemingly impervious self-confidence of this sophisticated woman dropped away to reveal the helplessness and despair of a lost little girl. She was completely unable to maintain her decorative brightness. She could not even muster a normalizing aside about knowing that she was not coping. Completely disarmed for the moment she could only despair: "I never learned how to get anyone to help me." I was touched by her helpless fall from grace.

Up till that moment I had just about decided to refer this seemingly shallow princess to some other therapist who would be more comfortable with her exaggerated pose of being so very special. Suddenly I found myself confronted with a substantial human being of unanticipated depths, an anguished woman filled with longing. Her controlling ways were more directed to constraining herself than to manipulating others. Though it would be complicated, I wanted to work with her. I told her just that.

Though *I* knew that my initial impatience had not been a ploy, she was understandably afraid to trust fully my earlier stated reluctance to take her on as a patient. Even so, she continued to do what she could to remain disarmed so that I might see more clearly the frightened unhappy private creature behind the grand-mannered public presentation.

Her display of good faith confirmed my decision to try to get to know her better if, after all this, *she* still wanted to continue the work with me. She said she would like to try to work out some way we could usefully spend time together. I assured her that she was welcome to bring along whatever measure of temporary distrust was needed to protect her from being needlessly hurt by me.

We began meeting regularly twice a week for psychotherapy sessions. Most of her energies went into trying to become my most very special patient. Exploration of her private anguish was reserved for rare moments when she could not bear the isolation of her royal posture of total self-sufficiency.

I invited reversal of these priorities by concentrating on the particular interventions that are called for during this opening phase of psychotherapy. My first task was the creation of an atmosphere of trust within which we could enter into a therapeutic alliance.

I begin by listening carefully to what a new patient has to say and to how it is said. I do not yet listen for the underlying dynamics that contribute to the patient's unhappiness. At the beginning, I am only trying to discover how it must feel to be that particular patient. For a while I do little more than try to formulate how the patient feels and to reflect those feelings back to the patient. It is enough that she finds that I am trying to understand how she experiences her life and that I help her to clarify her feelings without judging them.

This particular patient was used to being the center of attention. But having her feelings reflected without admiration or discounting was dramatically different from being continually groomed for the princess role. It was as though no one had ever before listened to what she had to say simply in order to try to understand how she felt. Instead she had been told how wonderful she was anytime she displayed her gifts of being bright, attractive, and obedient. Perhaps for the first time she realized clearly that all complaints of uncertainty, weakness, or unhappiness had been met by her adoring father's admonition: "Don't worry about that, my darling. You'll soon get over it. A wonderful girl like you can do anything."

Soon she revealed her fear that she had learned to impress people with more than she could deliver. She was sure that beneath her regal pose of competence and self-assurance, she was a shallow person who would eventually disappoint everyone. If she let anyone really get to know her, one day she would be exposed as an empty fraud who would interest no one. Because of this, it was desperately important to her to maintain her impressive aloofness, even at the cost of loneliness and unmet hunger for comforting of her hidden pain.

Another aspect of her style that was an unconscious way of guarding against father's loving demands was the development of what she called her "insightfulness." Her parenthetic running commentary on the rest of what she had to say turned out to be a way of escaping daddy's "making all her dreams come true."

As a child whenever she mentioned some object or activity that fit his projected image of her, daddy immediately arranged for her to have it or to do it. Once in her mid-teens offhandedly she repeated a friend's comment that Florence must be the most beautiful city in the world. Two weeks later, daddy announced that he had made all the arrangements for her trip to Italy that very summer.

Gradually she had learned never to reveal an inner thought or feeling without commenting on what it meant to her, lest someone transform that unguarded moment into an expensive long-term commitment. Her running commentary on her own remarks was an unconscious way of seeing to it that daddy knew when she really wanted something and when she was just musing.

During one session in the early months of our work together, unconsciously I entered into her old family drama. She was feeling hopeless about ever being able to give up playing out the role of the lonely princess, wishing she could know how her life would turn out. Instead of sticking with her through her despair, I offered the uncalled-for reassurance that she would someday be able to set aside her regal pose to reveal a substantial human being to whom some other people would be appreciatively responsive. She brightened visibly and demanded that I tell her more about it.

Unwittingly that session together we had recreated the entire complex configuration of Daddy and the Princess. I had given her the appreciation that she seemed to need. Without having to ask, she was given what she wanted without risking disappointment. But in order to get it she had to tolerate my discounting of her fears and to settle for what I thought was best for her.

In any case, the reassurance with which I mistakenly burdened her turned out to be less than she had in mind. No amount of reassurance could protect her from her self-doubt. Ironically, my self-serving belief in her simply made her more anxious about how much I expected in return. Again she had made too good a first impression. This only added to her certainty that she would turn out to be a disappointment.

Her reaction could have evoked more empty reassurances from me. They would certainly have encouraged her continuing spiral through another round of anxiety, demand, and deeper despair. Fortunately, once I recognized what I was inviting, I was able to shift into revealing myself. I told her of my own pampering and of the ways in which it contributed to my sometimes finding myself in her position. Supported by the mutual trust we had begun to build up, this shift of attention facilitated her being able to call on the sense of humor that more and more often allows her to laugh her way out of the traps that illusion invites.

It helped to free us both when she said, "We both think we're so special that we ought to be able to get along without any help or sympathy at all. All we need to do is to impress the whole world. *Noblesse oblige!*"

Certainly, had we each not suffered such painful contradictions in our childhood pampering, we might more easily have been able to comfort one another. Instead, momma's boy and daddy's little girl risked having to settle for sitting enthroned side by side, each innocently believing he or she was very special, and each needlessly feeling very much alone.

7

Pollyanna and the Paranoid

Insisting that you are someone special is just one of the ways of feeling needlessly isolated from other people. Maintaining oversimplified world-views may also keep a person out of touch with the everyday experiences that many others share.

Believing that things usually turn out bad is as naïve as believing that this is the best of all possible worlds. An overly optimistic Pollyanna attitude is simply a more obvious form of pseudo-innocence than a cynically paranoid outlook.

Both postures deny nature's indifference to the human situation. One person may imagine that there is someone out there watching over us. Another believes dark forces rule. Either extreme is an oversimplified view of life's ambiguities, an illusion of a unified coherent universe in which human beings hold a special central position. Beyond the limitation of that shared romantic assumption, each of these polar attitudes has its own advantages and disadvantages.

Having early assumed the semivoluntary/semiappointed office of family and community misfit, my own natural preference has usually been pessimistically paranoid. At times I am fully aware of the costs. I understand that my skepticism results in my passing up untried options that might have turned out to be wonderful opportunities. Often my distrust has led me out-of-hand to dismiss strangers who might have become my friends.

Even when I was conscious of what I might be losing out on, I was more likely to be impressed with the self-protective advantages and seeming good sense of my paranoia. For most of my life, I have believed that I lived in a dangerous world surrounded by untrustworthy people. In place of God, I projected a Perversity Principle, believing that if I really wanted something, I was sure *not* to get it, and if things went well for a while, catastrophe was imminent. In such a world, one would have to be crazy not to be a paranoid.[1]

The Pollyannas of this world live out the reverse side of this paranoid perspective. At times they may understand that their optimism often results in unexpected disappointments, and their gullibility in avoidable exploitation by others. But expecting that in the long run everything will turn out for the best, they go on trusting and trying, open to opportunities, seizing good luck, and rarely missing out on the joys that we paranoids sacrifice by playing it safe.

This mode of self-protective pseudo-innocence became my own style for much of my adult life. Ironically it was my first experience as a psychotherapy patient that helped me to develop my paranoid outlook. Bemuddled by years of immersion in an atmosphere of family hypocrisy, I had emerged from adolescence believing that I was an awful, inadequate human being who went around making other people unhappy. It was the only way I could account for being condemned by people as honest and good as my parents. I entered therapy to be cured of whatever failings had warranted their condemnation.

With the help of my first therapist, some of my problems were resolved. Some were not.

I learned to distinguish between my parents' chronic dissatisfaction and my having done something to deserve it. My guilt was resolved as I came to realize that just because they were critical did not necessarily mean that there was something wrong with me. It felt good not to be bad for a change. But with this joyful relief came the raw vulnerability of surrendering the illusion that if only I could be good, then my parents would treat me the way I always wished they had. As a hedge against fully experiencing that despair, I immersed myself in the mock-heroic pseudo-innocent fantasies that had earlier protected me against my losses of innocence. Not yet ready to accept the absence of fairness in life as it is, I became all the more determined to become the righteous avenger of injustice who would transform the world into what it should be. Undertaking such a quest meant being on my own against terrible odds. I alone would be beyond hypocrisy and deceit. Righting the wrongs and lighting the darkness, I would free the prisoners, rescue the victims, and punish the persecutors.

If not for yet another chance event in my randomly ordered life, this latest illusion might have come and gone as a harmless buffer temporarily put forward against the vulnerability of that therapeutic awakening. Unfortunately it was just at that phase of self-discovery that therapy was precipitously interrupted by my being drafted into the army. My therapist cautioned me about the emotional costs of not resuming the work when I was able, but high on my renewed illusion of living heroically I indulged in cluttering the next twenty years of my life with the melodramatic motif of imagining myself a good man in a bad world, threatened by the forces of darkness but ultimately protected by my own virtue and surely destined to live happily ever after, beginning someday soon.

Along the way I met other pseudo-innocents. Rather than choosing to be the hero, many of them preferred to have one. The resulting reciprocity gave me the opportunity to reinforce my illusion of being a specially significant human being. We played at giving and receiving the honor of being chosen. If they would appoint me their guru, I would accept them as my disciples.

At last I was honored for my understanding, appreciated for my goodness, and admired for my honest uncovering of evil. I had won. Though already long dead, my parents had been defeated.

And then one day the sky fell in. I had been chosen at random to undergo the fairy-tale shattering experience of suffering a brain tumor. Why me? I'd finally learned to be good. I had become the best. How could they do this to me?

The unfairness was too much to bear. I could not stand feeling so helplessly vulnerable again. I underwent neurosurgery. The operation was a partial success. I had survived with only limited handicaps but it was not possible to remove the tumor completely. It could grow again, require another bout of painful surgery and terrifying madness.

In any case I would die too soon. It seemed that there was nothing I could do about it. It was like being a child in my family all over again. I couldn't stand it. My heroic denials failed to obscure my helplessness.

I became deeply depressed. Residuals of my paranoia alienated me from the people who loved me and wanted to help. I would not put up with feeling trapped again. I would not live and die at the whim of cruel fate. I would overcome my helplessness. They would not get away with it this time. I decided to kill myself.

Later I wrote of that awful time in this way:

I felt a depth of helplessness and hopelessness that I had not experienced for more than twenty years, not since I was teen-aged, worthless, and lost.

Fear that the remaining sliver of tumor would begin to grow again left me feeling that, rather than someday simply dying, I was to be killed off. Or, worse yet, I felt the terror that I might not die, that instead I would become paralyzed. What would it be like to be trapped alive, imprisoned for years in a dead body? What if I could do nothing for myself, and if no one else would be there to bother to do for me, except out of burdensome pity?

I felt deeply sorry for myself. It seemed to me that I could not stand being so out of control of my life. My wife was there, with her own pain, and sorely open to mine. She later described it as "the summer we cried on the beach." But I was so into myself, so frightened, so determined to reassert my will and to have my own way that nothing else seemed to matter.

I spent many hours huddled on the empty beach, alone and brooding. Again and again, I decided that this was to be my final meeting with the sea, that I would swim out as far as I could, leaving my painful life, like a bundle of old clothes on the shore. And each time, I chose not to kill myself, explaining to myself that my wife and children needed me, would miss me too much. But it was not out of any sense of fairness to them that I did not drown myself. In my nearness to suicide, I really cared about nothing but escape from my own helplessness and anxiety. Recalling what I was up to, even now I still feel ashamed.

When we left the island to go home, I was still very depressed, unsure as to whether I was fit to help anyone else. It was time for me to get some help. But it was so very hard to face. I was feeling so down that the idea of going back into therapy as a patient once more made me feel like my life had been a fraud and a failure. And yet, if I would not go and ask something for myself, then everything I had tried to offer to my own patients was a lie.

There was an older therapist in town—a man whom I trust. He had supervised my work years ago, during a period when my father was dying. I used to go for supervision and cry every time. He had helped me then, and I hoped he would be able to help me again.

I phoned and told him briefly about my illness, and about how bad I finally realized I was feeling, hoping that he might have time free to see me. I was grateful and deeply moved when he told me he would "make time." The day I went to his office, I felt frightened, but was grimly determined to work things out. I told him my story in a detailed and well-organized account, and stated that I wanted to get to work right away, to get past this depression, to get back on my feet. Though sympathetic to the pain of my ordeal, his wry answer to my impatience was: "How come a big tough guy like you is thrown by a little thing like a brain tumor?" [2]

Feeling better after seeing him for a few consultations, I put off going on with the treatment I needed. Heroic still, I was determined to cure myself. After weeks of being very giving and considerate, my wife finally got openly angry. She was sorry I had to go through all this suffering, and troubled about my being so unhappy, but she was also fed up.

After she'd had enough, she told me: "Your paranoia is a pain in the neck. Your suspiciousness and irritability are making me and the kids miserable. I want you to do something about it. Not just for you, but for us too." I felt hurt and angry, but again her directness turned out to be enormously helpful.

I was stuck with my illness and being paranoid only made things worse. It was not true that this meant that I couldn't trust anyone or anything. No one was to blame. I had to learn to make peace with the arbitrariness of it all. Returning to therapy once more as a patient allowed me to begin accepting my helplessness with more grace. Once I could openly mourn my own promised early death, living with my losses no longer felt unbearable. More and more I became able to embrace uncomplainingly life's joyful moments. How much fuller these good times seemed once my attention was less divided by righteous insistence that this life was not enough.

My earlier experiences as a psychotherapy patient had changed my vision of my self. Until I was twenty I had believed that my family had shamed and punished me because I was a bad child who made everyone unhappy. With the help of my first therapist I gradually came to understand instead that the only reason I had been mistreated was because my mother hated me, and because my father did not care enough to intervene.

I redefined my personality style from guilt-ridden marginal delinquent to shamelessly righteous social reformer. Abandoning gambling, drugs, and streetwise hustling, I became a promising young graduate student. For the first time my grades reflected my considerable intelligence. After cleaning up my own act, I began brandishing the flaming sword of my super-integrity trip in a way that changed my reviews from panning to acclaim. I set out to rout the bad guys. Bad parents had scapegoated my innocent patients. As a therapist I would be a fairy godmother or the prince charming who would break the spell so that they might live happily ever after.

I made many errors and had my share of setbacks. Even so, twenty years later, I had become a successful professional. At worst, I had a somewhat controversial reputation as an unorthodox psychotherapist. Still, I was a long way from fulfilling the familial prophecy that I would end up in prison.

It was ironic. My professional and personal successes had confirmed my belief in fairy tales. Ready to get on with my own happily-ever-aftering, I was completely unprepared for the unfairness of facing catastrophic illness. Most of us take good health for granted. Unexpected illness evokes a certain natural measure of dismay from anyone. To that inevitable distress, I added the needless suffering of my pseudo-innocent protest that my falling ill was uncalled-for. Like Job, I demanded to know "Why me?" It wasn't fair, not after all the pain I had already endured. Not after I had devoted my adult life to being good. I refused to put up with the injustice of it all.

I fought to overcome the physical pain. The added tension only made it hurt all the more. Nor would I surrender to my grief. That stubborn denial transformed a sadness for which I might have sought comfort into depression from which there was no relief.

At the time I fell ill, I still believed that life had inherent meaning, and that I had an important part in what was to happen to me and to those around me. My tumor seemed an undeserved and tragic fate. How the hell did that fit into the grand scheme? Not only had I started out as the innocent victim of my parents' mistreatment. Nobly transcending that unfair disadvantage, I had gone on to transform my suffering into a continuing fight against injustice. Why should a good guy like me end up with a brain tumor?

It took almost two more years of therapy to resolve this pseudo-innocent question. Knowing that my mother had hated me was not enough. I remained excessively vulnerable to life's later random mishaps. I could not keep myself safe from making too much of my occasional bad luck until I realized that though it is probably true that my own mother hated me, it was *nothing personal.*

Any kid living in that house at that time would have served as a suitable target. It was my misfortune to have been the one who wandered in. There was no special meaning to it all, no compensations for that less-than-perfect beginning. As an adult I was free to choose to do what I could to alleviate the suffering of others. I need only do so, understanding that this humane activity would neither avenge my past nor assure my future.

The first time I entered therapy my question had been, "Why am I such an awful person?" The answer turned out to be, "You are not an awful person. You only feel that way now because as a child you were treated as though you were bad." This time my question was, *"Why me?"* The answer turned out to be, *"Why not?"*

The playfulness of this reply made room for my beginning to live a more antic life, a life freer of the burdensome expectations of meaning, reason, and fairness. Still it seems to me that I am not yet done with all of my paranoia. Like other forms of pseudo-innocence, its persistence inheres mainly in giving fairy-tale meaningfulness to the purposeless suffering provided by life's random evils. By encouraging an avenging stance in what seems like the worst of all possible worlds, the paranoid attitude does offer vigilance against those who would do me harm.

Unfortunately, my paranoia also leads me to confuse feeling scared with being in danger, and to hurt others who are really friendly or merely indifferent. What's more, the exotic flowering of paranoia is demonic. It gets out of hand too easily. There are pseudo-innocent neurotics whose paranoid character style is not ever likely to reach delusional proportions. Even so, a high price must be paid emotionally for the maintaining of this self-protectively cynical outlook. I treated such a man some years ago. Although bright, accomplished, and engagingly charming when not affecting his paranoid vigilance, he came to therapy because whatever joy came into his life seemed sure to be spoiled.

He had been depressed for years. Good things always turned out badly in his relationships with other people. In the whining of his discontent I began to hear his stinginess, his envy, and his distrust. He had many long stories to tell about people who had let him down or had tried to do him in. Again and again he self-righteously relished proving that someone else was to blame for his unhappiness. It was almost as though it was worth feeling miserable so long as he could be sure that it was someone else's fault.

Slowly he became more and more aware and acknowledging of this self-destructive paranoid pattern of his joyless interactions with other people. But it was not until he acted it out with me that he experienced the vulnerability from which it protected him. He and I seemed to have established some basis for mutual trust. We had exchanged accounts of the personal experiences that had made each of us somewhat paranoid and had agreed to trust our distrust whenever that seemed the thing to do.

It was during these weeks of newfound ease and intimacy that he tried to get me to spoil our relationship. Though he knew in advance that the policy offered no coverage for preexisting conditions, he signed up for an expensive health insurance plan. Then he let me know that the only way that he would be able to continue to afford to pay for psychotherapy was if I would agree to falsify his insurance claim form so that the company would be misled into believing that he had just begun seeing me.

At first I misunderstood this maneuver to be his attempt to find out if I cared enough to lie for him. We struggled for a few sessions to uncover what his tempting me was all about. Pouting and complaining, he insisted that this was simply his way of trying to ease his financial burdens so that he could afford to continue to see me. I would not respond to his insistence that this was a situational administrative problem. Treating his behavior as unconsciously determined, I neither granted nor denied his request. Instead I left him frustrated and hating me, offering him only psychological interpretations.

At last he understood what was going on. He let me know that I was mistaken in believing that he had been testing my love by trying to find out whether or not I would lie for him. We had gotten *too* close. Terrified by his vulnerability in the relationship, he had set out to prove that I was no more to be trusted than all the others. If I was taken in and willing to participate in that fraudulent contract, then he would know for sure that I was as corrupt as everyone else, that nothing but the money mattered to me either.

Now he realized that I would not take his offer seriously. Instead, even at the risk of losing him, I had insisted on fulfilling my commitment of doing the work that promised to enhance his understanding of himself. His own response to my behavior ranged from disbelief, through petulance, to an enormous sense of relief at not being able to trick me into doing him in. But with that relief came the dammed up anguish of so many isolated years of loneliness and secret longing. He cried that day for a long, long time. We had to live out this pattern many more times before it became clear enough for him to be free of his needless suffering much of the time.

Whether successful or unsuccessful, paranoia is a dangerous defense. Even so, for me, believing that this is the worst of all possible worlds remains a more appealing exaggeration than its counterpart. If pseudo-innocent I must be, better a paranoid than a Pollyanna. During my most cynical phase, when I trusted no one but my fellow paranoids, I avoided all those who insisted that this was the *best* of all possible worlds. It was exactly the right time for me to come upon Voltaire's satirical novel *Candide*.[3]

The title character seemed a caricature of just the sort of optimistic innocence I hated most in so many other young people of my age. Candide's teacher, Pangloss, had taught him to believe that ultimate goodness and divine fairness were the underlying causes of every apparent evil. Pangloss reminded me of all the older people whom I detested at the time. They always seemed to be telling me to trust those who knew better. "Someday, you'll see," they would promise. "It may not make sense to you right now, but in the end everything always works out for the best."

Painfully, Candide comes at last to lose his innocence. He is exposed to destruction beyond human control in the form of plagues, earthquakes, and other natural disasters. Even the social calamities he must face are so vast that he can find no one to blame, and nothing to redeem the suffering they cause. Beyond the sweeping disasters of war and poverty, Candide witnesses random individual pain as he learns that both fortune and misfortune fall upon the good as indiscriminately as they do on the wicked.

Voltaire was an outspoken skeptic and a dedicated practical moralist. He viewed life as neither good nor bad, but rather as tolerably mediocre. The few sweet experiences in this world provide occasional relief from the otherwise uninterrupted stream of misery and wretchedness. These moments of good fortune and kindness provide sufficient joy to make one often feel that it is worthwhile after all. At such times, it is not necessary to assume that suffering is all for the best in order to feel that life is worth living.

Like Candide, some of my patients come to therapy burdened by needless disappointments resulting from their pseudo-innocent insistence that *this is the best of all possible worlds.* Their short-sighted denials remind me of the old joke about the optimistic son of sadistic parents. One Christmas morning, opening the presents they had given him, he discovered that each was a gift-wrapped box of manure. Instead of getting upset, he ran around excitedly poking into the basement, the closets, and the attic. His cruel parents were bewildered until they heard him shouting gleefully, "If there's that much horseshit here, there must be a pony around somewhere!"

I explain to some of these patients that they suffer from *Narapoia.* This pathological exaggeration of a simpler and more functional Pollyanna attitude becomes an inverted form of paranoia, characterized by the delusional belief that people are out to help you. Narapoids do little to take care of themselves beyond trying harder and harder to please the people who treat them badly. The more coldly detached their lovers, the more trustingly narapoids cling to them. Some of these patients are men, but most are women. Our male-dominated culture does much to maintain its sexist power structure by selectively encouraging women to believe in this particular brand of pseudo-innocence.

Women seek the help of psychotherapists more frequently than men do. Perhaps their greater optimism is one of the reasons accounting for the discrepancy. Paradoxically, when they find the understanding and consideration they seek, such women usually become very uncomfortable. They seem more ready to receive the criticism that they believe is needed to straighten them out. Some fear only that they will not be sufficiently pleasing to be allowed to remain in therapy long enough to be properly disciplined.

I get the feeling that such a patient would trust me more readily if I were to confront her harshly, demanding immediate "improvement." My acceptance of her *as she is* is much harder for her to tolerate. The fact that I take her seriously and am concerned about what she feels is so unexpected as to be almost disorienting. It has taken me a long while to begin to understand why the naïvely optimistic patient should back away from the kindness she purportedly seeks and expects.

Recently a woman patient suffering from narapoia tearfully described her unsuccessful efforts to satisfy an inconsiderately demanding and often unreliable male "friend." She ended her telling of the vignette with unjustly harsh self-condemnation: "I guess I'm just not interesting enough for him to bother wasting his time on me." Narapoids are usually found attached to unkind lovers. Characteristically they are understanding of others' cruelty.

I responded with a simple reflection of her feelings: "He's never there when you need him. You believe that it must be because you don't have enough to offer." Feeling understood, she was able to go on to amplify her account of what a wonderful world it would be were it not for her inadequacy.

When she had told me enough to warrant the interpretation, I offered, "You're so very hard on yourself. You live in a fantasy world in which you insist goodness is always rewarded. And so when you don't get what you want, you blame yourself." At first she resisted by absorbing my remarks into the bog of her self-degradation. "You're right. I guess I'm very stupid. Maybe if I tried harder—"

I interrupted. "You pull away from experiencing my concern about how very hard you are on yourself. If things don't turn out well, you insist that it must be your fault. It's so easy for you to go on blaming yourself. You find it hard to join me in considering that your 'friend' is as impossible to satisfy as your father was. Neither of them ever appreciated how much you give of yourself."

Clearly she was touched by what I was saying, but overwhelmed by her own response. Blinking away the tears and choking down the sobs, she tried to go on making out a case for self-improvement. If only she read up on the subjects that interested her friend, he might treat her better.

Again I intervened. "You're feeling that I'm being too kind to you. When you finally sense that someone does appreciate you, you feel so vulnerable that you can hardly stand the pain. It's then that you know that no matter how hard you try, no matter how good you are, some of the men who are most important to you will never ever appreciate you."

This time she sobbed openly for a long, long time. The anguished sound of each wrenching cry heralded the loss of one more bit of innocence. At last she had begun to wonder: If this is the best of all possible worlds, then what must the others be like?

In the long run, the pseudo-innocence of being a Pollyanna works no better than that of being a paranoid. Pop psychology assures us all that we can live happily ever after. Still, for some of us the doubts persist. The Smothers Brothers do a comedy routine in which Tommy, having just returned from an encounter-group weekend workshop, assails Dick with his newfound key to happiness: "I'm okay. You're okay." [4] He goes on and on enthusiastically only to falter finally into the pleading inquiry, "You are okay, aren't you?"

Avenging paranoids like me are tempted to waste our lives in self-righteous justification. "I'm okay but you're not okay," we insist.

Paranoids and Pollyannas alike, we might all best devote ourselves to accepting human imperfection, and trying to make the best of this unjust life as it is. If we formed a club, the lettering on the backs of our jackets might read: I'M NOT O.K. YOU'RE NOT O.K. AND THAT'S O.K." [5]

8

Too Good to Be True

Both the paranoid and the Pollyanna are preoccupied mainly with what is going on outside of themselves. We may infer that each of these pseudo-innocent social postures also serves to divert attention away from unacceptable aspects of inner life.

Certainly the paranoid's projections attribute to others motives too bad to be accepted as belonging to the self. And the Pollyanna's naïve demand for a world so caring and protective that it will never be disappointing implies a vision of a self worthy enough to deserve a life in which everything always works out for the best.

Even so, the primary focus of both of these attitudes is the behavior of others and the outcome of external events. There is another breed of pseudo-innocent whose attention is directed mainly toward the maintaining of a saintly self-image. As a strategy for living, saintliness may have its own implicitly exploitive expectations of how others are to respond to one's purity. Still, the main concern is with continuing reassurance of one's own angelic innocence. I find that such people always turn out to be too good to be true.

Some of my earliest professional experiences contributed to this observation. Later clinical and personal encounters continue to support it. Earlier in this book [1] I described my innocently mock-heroic first visit to a building for the criminally insane. That fragment of my education as a youthfully underripe and sometimes needlessly foolish naïf was preceded by two other experiences with "sane" criminal inmates in nonpsychiatric correctional institutions.

At age twenty-two I began my first placement as a psychology intern at the New Jersey State Reformatory at Bordentown, a custodial setting for male felons aged sixteen to thirty. In retrospect, I feel that at that age, I had no business serving on the staff of a reformatory, not even in the apprentice role of intern. At twenty-two, in many ways, I was still an emotional virgin. I dressed and acted hip and tough, but I was a lamb in wolf's clothing. The inmates sized me up easily and correctly. They intimidated me. They conned me. They manipulated me. They turned me every way but loose.

The inmate population was made up largely of young men who had a record of no more than one or two "serious" convictions. Considered potentially rehabilitatable, they served indeterminate sentences. This meant that each man's "progress" was formally reviewed twice a year, and that depending on the results of those evaluations, he could be released at any six-month interval within the span of his maximum sentence.

Part of my job was to participate in these evaluations. The only redeeming factor was that the administrative staff probably put little stock in my unseasoned judgments. The inmates used a variety of ploys to influence my rating of their progress. Some parroted psychoanalytic insights about the influence of their unhappy childhoods. Others confided in me as if I were the only member of the staff who really understood. One of the less polished inmates offered to teach me how to crack a safe. Many of them simply hinted darkly that something awful might happen to me if I let them down. One man's threat amounted to no more than his reminding me that I should know him pretty well because working in the staff dining room he was the one who daily chose which bowl of soup to serve me.

I made those judgments as independently of the flattery, con jobs, and intimidation as I knew how. But even when my judgments were objective in that sense, they remained meaningless. What did I know about predicting future criminal behavior? I understood little of the men whom I presumed to judge. I appreciated nothing of what it meant to be locked up and deprived of freedom. Those men and that place terrified me, and my concern with proving myself demanded that I deny that it was all far more than I was yet prepared to manage.

My first day on the job, I did my best to ignore my impression that practically every inmate looked like a thug who might murder me just for the fun of it. They all reminded me of those street-corner hoods I had encountered so many times as a kid.

Whenever I ventured out of my own neighborhood on an errand, not looking for trouble, just minding my own business, I always seemed to run into one of these guys. Inadvertently I would make momentary eyeball contact with some young tough who was idly lounging up against a corner candystore newstand. He might be doing no more than grabbing a free read of the *News* and *Mirror,* but in my later recollections he always seemed to have been casually cleaning his nails with a Bowie knife.

No matter how inoffensive my attitude, no matter who this particular bully might be, his taunting greeting to me was always the same. Each time the singsong accusation was issued once again in the form of that devastatingly unanswerable question: "What do you think *you're* looking at?" The first few times I attempted a friendly denial. But when I answered, "Nothing," he countered, "You sayin' I'm nothing?" And if I tried to clarify my message: "I meant I wasn't looking at you," he was sure to rechallenge with "Are you calling me a liar?"

It was just no use. He would always push me into a fight. No matter how large or small that particular bully, I always got beaten up. I had meant no harm. I could never quite believe that he would beat me up for nothing. If I had learned at that age to give up the expectation that my innocence would protect me, I would have hit him in the mouth as soon as he challenged me. That would have been that. But I was still too young and too sincere to protect myself that ruthlessly.

When I entered the reformatory, had I acknowledged how many of the inmates reminded me of those unmanageable challengers, I would have fled the institution, overwhelmed with terror. Instead I accounted for my uneasiness as a kind of culture shock. It was still a foreign environment. The inmates looked like people from some very poor neighborhood, uneducated, lower class, perhaps simply Gentile.

Desperately, I grasped at the reassuring realization that there were a few exceptions. Wandering around, uncertain about where to get the materials I needed, just what my territory might be, and lacking any real sense of how things worked within the reformatory, I did encounter three or four very appealing inmates. Each in his own way was helpful, sympathetic, and cooperative. Each seemed like a sweet guy. I could not for the life of me understand what the hell nice guys like that were doing locked up in a place like this.

At the end of the day I talked to one of the older staff members. Considerately, he had asked me how I was doing and had given me a chance to talk. Rather than make use of the opportunity to express my anxiety, I waxed philosophical, discoursing heavily regarding my conception of what criminal reform was all about.

He smiled indulgently, telling me that when I was a little less scared, I might be able to talk about just how scared I really was. Paradoxically, his accepting way of penetrating my facade led me to describe to him those rare inmates who had *not* frightened me. When I told about the behavior of these few sweet guys and of my bewilderment as to what they might be doing there, he was quickly able to identify them by physical description and to tell me their names. I could not understand how he was able to recognize immediately who it was I had been describing as having been so helpful. His startling explanation was, "Oh sure, they're all the same, sweetest guys in any prison. Every one of them is in for murder."

He went on to explain that these were people least likely to repeat their crime. Usually murderers were given long sentences and treated as though they were a continuing menace to society. Instead, each of these men was the sort described by neighbors as polite, cooperative, inoffensive. Everyone who knew them was startled when one day one of these sweetly pseudo-innocent characters suddenly shot and killed his wife. Without warning another had cut his cousin to death with a broken bottle following a minor disagreement. A third had taken a baseball bat to a neighbor's head. Up to the point of that homicidal outburst of violence, each had seemed a vision of goodness. Right after the murder, each had surrendered to the police without a struggle, pleaded guilty with regret, and thrown himself on the mercy of the court. Each was accepting and understanding of the long maximum sentence that the law required. Within each man's saintly appearance was a long-denied and consequently exaggerated natural capacity for brutality. After the outburst of homicidal violence, each resumed the chronic pseudo-innocent posture that had indeed turned out to be too good to be true.

After completing that segment of my internship, I was given a second placement, this time at a state mental hospital. When I finished my year's internship, I was then "qualified" to accept a staff position. I was hired as a clinical psychologist at the New Jersey State Prison at Trenton, a maximum-security institution for adult male felons, who were usually multiple offenders considered too hardened to warrant reformatory status or indeterminate sentencing.

This job lasted only three months before I was drafted into the army. But during even so short a time, again I discovered that almost all of the prison inmates convicted of murder were sweet helpful first offenders. They had been sent to the prison only because they were too old to be housed in the reformatory.[2]

By this time I looked back on my unsuccessful efforts to rehabilitate the reformatory inmates as the simple consequence of my lack of technical skill as an intern. Innocently I had come to believe that now that my good intentions were backed up by a full year of training and credentials and by my postinternship professional status, I was ready to be the wonderfully healing presence I longed to become.

I was fortunate to find myself working for a prison warden who was far less innocent than I. The warden was a rather remarkable man. He held a Ph.D. in sociology and had long been a well-known specialist in criminal behavior. Despite his doctoral degree, he looked like an ex-prizefighter, and sometimes he acted like one.

Among the inmates he had the reputation of being tough but fair. Under duress, he had been known to set aside his Ph.D., pick up an automatic rifle, and quell a fomenting riot by firing over the heads of the menacing mob of inmates. Another time, he had to contend with a powerful assaultive inmate who, during a psychotic episode, had barricaded himself in a solitary cell. Armed with a home-made knife, the prisoner was able to fend off the guards' efforts to contain his rage and transfer him to the hospital for the criminally insane. According to all accounts, the warden had entered the cell unarmed and talked this homicidal madman into handing over his weapon and going along quietly to the hospital.

I'd been hired by the chief staff psychologist. My first day on the job we had passed the warden in the hallway and my department head introduced us with no more than a formal exchange of names and titles. The warden told me that he would give me a chance to learn my way around before we got together to talk.

I'd been working at the prison for almost three weeks before I was summoned to his office. It was a smaller room than I'd expected, fitted with all the furniture and equipment he might absolutely need, but completely free of frills.

Alone with the warden in his office, I'd hardly gotten seated when he demanded, "In your professional opinion would psychoanalysis keep these men from repeating their criminal behavior?"

Believing that if he had a question then I must have an answer, I responded as though I understood the problem. "I'm sure that some of these problems are social in origin and require political rather than psychological solutions. Even so it seems to me that re-habilitative psychotherapy should be of real value in changing the lives of most of these men."

"What about Duke Donelli?" he challenged. "Is he a suitable candidate for rehabilitative psychotherapy?"

Joseph "Duke" Donelli was a "new fish," a recently committed inmate. I had had no direct contact with him, but like everyone else at the prison, I knew who he was. For years he had served as one of organized crime's chief lieutenants. After the federal government's tax-evasion conviction of his boss, Duke had taken over the running of illegal gambling operations in the state. Many years later the state government had finally been able to lock him up on a charge of bribery.

All I could muster to ward off the warden's challenge was the excuse that I had not yet had a chance to look over the man's folder or to interview him. I would have to reserve any clinical judgment.

The warden's sardonic smile let me know that neither one of us believed my preposterous posturing. In his own way, he was kind about it: "I believe you're right that many of the inmates' problems are social and only some psychological. In my opinion, because of the effects of social conditions that spawned them, almost all of the men in this institution will be back, no matter what we do with them here. If there are a few that we can change, with counseling or any other method, I'd appreciate your working on the problem of how to identify which of the men have personality problems underlying their criminal behavior.

"As for an administrative type like Donelli, our only problem will be to see to it that he doesn't take over and run the inmate population. In my opinion he is about as psychologically disturbed as a vice president of General Motors, and in just about the same ways. If you think that psychotherapy would result in his counterpart quitting his executive post at G.M., then I guess you would expect counseling to effect a career change in Donelli, providing he's in the midst of an identity crisis."

There seemed little more to say for the moment. I was relieved when he dismissed me.

Some weeks later, once more the warden sent for me. Again he asked how I was doing, and again I lied, saying that I was doing fine. He returned to the issue of selection of inmates for psychotherapy and for recommendation for release by the parole board. "I understand that you've been doing a great deal of psychological testing. How helpful do you believe that program will prove in accurately predicting inmate behavior in the community after release?"

This time I felt prepared. I'd thought a lot about these screening procedures and had discussed the problem with a number of other clinical psychologists. It might even turn out to be a workable topic for my doctoral dissertation.

In my first contest with the warden, I had been unsure of myself. This time I felt a confidence solidly based on well-reasoned discussion (if not yet on extensive experience): "While not always accurate, these test results definitely are informative. I figure that to be useful my predictions only need to be statistically better than chance. Any time they are, I will have saved the state a great deal of money, and have given some human being a new lease on life. All I have to do to earn my pay is to be able to make the right decision at least half of the time."

This time the warden didn't smile. "Your job demands decisions every day about men so dangerous that the community keeps them locked up in cages. You think you're doing fine if you're right at least half the time. If one of my guards told me that, I'd fire him."

I staggered out of the warden's office. Here was yet another shock wave of life as it is. Once again I had been robbed of the soothing illusion that my understanding and good intentions were sufficient to make things right. Faced with the seriousness of having to deal with the seemingly unsolvable problems of brutality and violence brought a rush of awareness that I experienced simultaneously as both new and yet familiar.

Again there was that disturbing discovery that every time I learned something important, instead of a sense of gain I first experienced a deep sense of loss. This new piece of instruction on the impossibility of eradicating evil took me back several years to a quiet summer evening at Pete's Place, the neighborhood poolroom in which I had spent so many sheltered adolescent hours.

I was seventeen and alone in the city. All the other guys in my crowd were musicians who had taken summer jobs playing in Catskill resort bands. I was practicing billiards by myself when a quiet little guy perhaps a year or two older than I came to the table. He waited until I stopped shooting and then asked me softly if I was Shelly Kopp. I said, sure, and asked him what he wanted. In an appealing way he said that it was private stuff and would I mind coming outside to talk a bit. I was kind of bored anyway and my stroking wasn't going too well, so I said, "Sure, why not?"

Once outside I quickly found myself surrounded by six or eight guys who looked a hell of a lot bigger and tougher than the messenger they had sent to get me. They herded me around the corner and into the darkness of an empty side street.

I was terribly frightened but assured myself that because I hadn't done anything to hurt anyone, nothing dreadful would happen to me. It turned out that the leader of this group was the boyfriend of a teen-age girl whom I had dated casually. He had heard from yet another girl that I had claimed that his girlfriend was one of my sexual conquests. As a matter of fact, in my adolescent macho way I had simply spoken ambiguously about our relationship hoping that I would sound like a stud.

In any case I denied it all. I said that certainly I knew the girl and I respected her and that if I had been understood to say anything offensive about her then surely I had been misunderstood. This tough bunch seemed to be in the mood to get on with it anyway. The implication was that my having spoken "out of line" about this girl was grounds for a rumble. They wanted to know what gang I belonged to and where my "boys" were. I smiled weakly explaining that I belonged to no gang at all, that my boys were musicians who were spending the summer out of town playing in hotel bands, and that even if there was a fight not one of them would have taken part for fear of risking his embouchure.

They seemed unable to believe that I was without pride. There was no challenge they might offer that I could not absorb smilingly. I don't know if they finally believed what I had told them, or if they simply could not believe the sort of a wimp they had encountered. In any case these toughs wandered off shaking their heads, warning me that I had better never do what they had heard that I had done.

Briefly I had been afraid they might really hurt me, but they hadn't. During the next few days again and again I replayed the scene in my head, revising it to reassure myself that the worst that could have happened was that I might have gotten a bloody nose or some other minor injury. Besides, I believed that if you don't really do anything bad then nothing awful will happen to you anyway. It wouldn't be fair.

One evening the next week I was standing on the street corner where unattached teen-agers hung out. With a squeal of brakes an old Chevy pulled up at the curb. It was the Moose. "Shelly, my main man, hop in my short."

When the Moose said, "Hop," people hopped. I was the only one in the neighborhood for whom it might have been safe not to respond, but I never risked taking the option.

Moose, as everybody called him, was a powerfully built, violently tempered young man of seemingly unlimited strength and obviously limited intelligence. He had been known to punch out anyone who made him angry.

He never menaced me. We had grown up together. When we were still little kids, I had once bested him in a schoolyard scuffle. Seemingly unaware of the growing disparities in our physical as well as our mental developments, since that day a decade earlier, he persisted in thinking of me as "the only dude in the neighborhood who could take the Moose in a fair fight."

As soon as I got into the car, we sped off. He pulled up to the curb and parked on a deserted street. Only then did he tell me the story that had been so hard for him to hold back behind his self-satisfied, dumb, sweet smile.

"Shelly, my man, Saturday night I was partying with some bad faces over in the East Bronx. One of them was jumping Western about some cat from my neighborhood who bad-mouthed his best buddy's chick. He started waving his piece around, saying he should have shot the bastard when they pulled him out of Pete's last week. And you know what? I wouldn't shit you, my man. The dude he was gonna dust turned out to be you!"

I couldn't take it all in. A gun. How could I believe that one of those toughs that night had been carrying a real gun? I would have been tempted to believe that Moose had made up the story, only I knew he was too dumb to lie. At any rate, in moments all my doubts were settled.

"Open up the glove compartment," he commanded.

I hesitated.

"Open it, my man," he urged impatiently.

Coming to my senses, I quickly turned the knob releasing the catch that allowed the front of the compartment to drop open.

"It's in there," he said insistently. "Dig it, man. Did you think it wouldn't be in there? Go on, take it out!"

I reached around in the darkness of the open glove compartment. When I brought out my hand, there was a gun in it. I couldn't believe that all of this was happening to me.

"I wouldn't let anyone hassle *you,* Shelly. I took the piece away from that big-mouthed creep. I told him nobody messes with the Moose's main man."

For all my stuporous terror, I managed to thank him for saving my life. He loved it.

"You keep the piece," he told me.

"No, Moose, that's all right. I appreciate all you've done for me. Why don't you keep the gun? Maybe you could sell it or something."

He smiled the specially warm childlike smile he reserved for someone who would be kind to the Moose even though he knew he could take him in a fair fight. "Hey, thanks a lot, Shelly. I can use the bread. You're my main man, my mainest man."

He dropped me off back at our regular street-corner hangout. I went on into the candy store and ordered the usual (a chocolate egg cream and a piece of halvah). The counter was crowded. I went to the back and sat down in a booth to try to think this through. Suddenly I saw that all bets were off. Life was a game in which the rules had been changed. Kid-time was over. Getting into a fight could mean a lot more than risking a black eye or a bloody nose. Now it was real, like in the movies. Real guns, with bullets. Bang! Bang! You're dead, and that's all she wrote. No getting up and saying, "Now you be the bad guy." No getting up at all.

I had to learn to keep my mouth shut. I had to understand that no matter how good you were, there were dangerous people in this world who just might kill you. I had to learn that whole thing. I just had to.

The macho guy with the gun was one kind of romantic innocent. The Moose was another. I was a third. In his own way each of us risked bringing violence down on himself and on those around him. Not all the murderers of this world are sweet, and not all those of us who play it too-good-to-be-true turn out to be sweet murderers. Yet in its own way pseudo-innocence encourages evil and destruction. Supergood intentions often result in superbad actions.

Seemingly pure innocents usually do turn out to be too good to be true. Billy Budd is the classic literary example of a saintly character who becomes an unexpected menace mainly because of his denial of the existence of destructive forces both within himself and in the world about him.

This British "Handsome Sailor" was the memorable hero of Herman Melville's long short story [3] about the young foretopman's fall from grace. Billy's manner was as flawlessly virginal and angelic as his appearance. Admired by almost everyone, while faithfully carrying out his duties, he managed to create an atmosphere of goodwill and affection among almost all his shipmates.

The story takes place toward the end of the eighteenth century, at a time when the British navy was threatened with losing its command of the seas. Ordinary seamen lived and worked under conditions so oppressive that their discontent finally flared up into a series of short-lived mutinies. Even after these insurrections had been quelled, the danger of new uprisings kept the officers uneasily vigilant without yet convincing them to redress the men's grievances.

It became difficult to man the ships. With fewer and fewer voluntary enlistments, the admiralty found it necessary to resume the old abandoned custom of impressment. Press gangs literally kidnapped young men off the streets. Officers of heavily gunned warships took whatever sailors they chose from the crews of merchant vessels they encountered at sea.

So it was that Billy Budd came to be transferred by impressment from the homeward-bound merchant ship *Rights-of-Man* to the battle-seeking man-of-war HMS *Indomitable*. His simplicity and innocence unshaken by this disruption, unprotestingly Billy moved from one ship to the other. With all but cheerful acquiescence once more he had accepted unquestioningly whatever life set before him.

Once transferred, he continued to do all that was expected of him with goodhumored enthusiasm and unstinting generosity. Had he bothered to pay attention to such matters, he soon would have noticed that once again he had become the darling of the men among whose hammocks he swung his own. He might have realized as well that he had found favor even in the eyes of Captain Vere, a man who ran his own life by devotion to justice and his ship by obedience to the law.

But Billy made little attempt to evaluate the meaning of his experiences. For him, all things were what they seemed. Accepting life without reflection, he went along with it without complaint. Honest and open-hearted, he expected that everyone else was the same and that all was right with the world. Though popular with almost everyone he met, and as strong as he was beautiful, Billy was the least worldly of men. An illiterate foundling, "ignorant of even who his father was . . . [Billy was as] unself-conscious . . . [as] young Adam before the Fall." [4]

He lacked any understanding of malice and would have been baffled by the idea of devious motives. Just as his innocence kept him unaware of the dark and turbulent side of himself, it blinded him to evidence of the potential for evil in others. Denials so massive left him more than vulnerable to the destructive wiles of more worldly men.

By playing into the jaded cynicism of the ship's master-at-arms, Billy's stubborn innocence made him an unwitting accomplice to their mutual destruction. As master-at-arms, it was Claggart's duty to maintain discipline among the common seamen. This he accomplished through a willful combination of stealth and force, manipulating deviously where he could, and brutalizing savagely when he had to.

Young Billy retained the innocent purity of heart that the older man had so long ago lost. Left only with his own bitter cynicism, Claggart hated Billy for his faith. Denying his envy of Billy's simple trusting ways, the master-at-arms felt only contempt for the young fool whose downfall he would bring about.

Again and again, Claggart set minor obstacles and petty problems in Billy's path. Even when older sailors tried to help Billy to recognize Claggart's gratuitous mischief for what it was, Billy simply could not believe that anyone he'd done no harm would want to hurt him.

Finally on a night so warm that Billy chose to sleep on deck, Claggart sent another impressed sailor to entrap Billy as a conspirator to mutiny. But Billy could neither hear evil nor speak it. Interrupting the fellow before he could make things perfectly clear, Billy began to stutter as he always did when his own unacceptable anger began to emerge: " 'D-d-damme, I don't know what you are d-d-driving at, or what you mean, but you had better g-g-go where you belong!' " [5]

Unfortunately, being the innocent that he was, Billy did not act forcefully enough to protect himself. Not wanting to hurt anyone's feelings, he never did answer clearly, "NO, I will not participate in planning a mutiny," nor did he consider informing on his fellow shipmate.

Ironically, blinded by the light of his own unquestioning innocence, Billy had left himself vulnerable to being cast in the shadow of Claggart's accusation of guilt. Ordered to report to Captain Vere's cabin, Billy could only imagine that he had been summoned to receive some reward for being good.

Instead he found himself denounced by Claggart for allegedly taking part in planning a mutiny. At first Billy could not take it in. Overwhelmed by the injustice of the accusation, he could only stammer incomprehensibly.

Captain Vere urged him to speak out and defend himself. Then realizing that his urging had only aggravated the young sailor's helpless stammering, the captain tried to soothe Billy by encouraging him to take his time.

But this expression of fatherly concern only made matters worse. The older man's kindness moved Billy to try harder to have his say. At the same time Claggart's unjust accusation filled him with impotent rage for which he could find no words. Caught between the two, he could not speak at all.

Then all at once Billy's lifelong mask of easygoing innocence was torn away to reveal the turbulent aspect that he had till then hidden even from himself: " . . . quick as the flame from a discharged cannon at night, his right arm shot out, and Claggart dropped to the deck [dead]." [6]

Despite his sympathy and affection for Billy, for Captain Vere the law was the law. He had no choice: "Struck dead by an angel of God! Yet the angel must hang!" [7] There followed a simple and summary drumhead court. Billy accepted his sentence like a child who understands that others know what is best for him.

The following dawn, Billy was to be hanged from the mainyard. So that they too might be instructed, the entire crew was ordered out to witness his execution. Innocent to the last, just before he was strung up, without a trace of a stammer, Billy shouted out: "God bless Captain Vere!" [8]

Few of the too-good-to-be-true innocents of this world literally become sweet murderers or even unwittingly encourage holocausts. Still, to the extent that they deny the existence of evil forces in themselves and others, again and again in his or her own way each unwittingly abets socially or personally destructive transactions with the people around them. Getting to know such people has taught me to distrust seemingly pure goodness. It may seem strange for me to say that we need to be afraid of goodness. Instead, should we not fear evil?

Folly is a more dangerous enemy to the good than evil. One can protest against evil; it can be unmasked and, if need be, prevented by force. Evil always carries the seeds of its own destruction, as it makes people, at the least, uncomfortable. Against folly we have no defense. Neither protests nor force can touch it; reasoning is no use; facts that contradict personal prejudices can simply be disbelieved—indeed, the fool can counter by criticizing them, and if they are undeniable, they can just be pushed aside as trivial exceptions. So the fool, as distinct from the scoundrel, is completely self-satisfied; in fact, he can easily become dangerous, as it does not take much to make him aggressive. A fool must therefore be treated more cautiously than a scoundrel; we shall never again try to convince a fool by reason, for it is both useless and dangerous.[9]

Unhappy at the outcome of their folly, some of the neurotic too-good-to-be-true innocents end up seeking psychotherapy. The ones who seek my help have not been sent by the courts. Few begin by complaining about guilt experienced because of awareness of their own destructive behavior.

Most of them suffer from depression. But it is not that sorrowful feeling about themselves and their lives that brings them to my office. Instead most often they seek help only because they find it insufferable to have discovered that they are upset. Recognition of their depression means that they are flawed and may be rejected. They see their illusion of perfection as damaged and in need of repair. They come to therapy in a hurry to get over this depression that is spoiling their otherwise wonderful lives.

One such angelic pseudo-innocent described her need for therapy in the following way:

My husband says I'm going crazy. I'm sure he must be right or I wouldn't have been acting so upset for the last few months. I have fits of crying when there's absolutely no reason in the world for me to be unhappy.

After all, I have everything any woman could want. My husband is a very prominent attorney. He's polite and considerate. Everyone who meets him thinks he's a really nice person, always reliable, and very reasonable.

We have two lovely children. He's given me a beautiful house in the suburbs. We have our own swimming pool and the kids even get to go to private school.

What do I have to be depressed about? I have so much more than most other people. What some women wouldn't give to have the perfect life that I get to have.

This depression is ugly. I've become a bother to my husband and to all of the other people who care about me. I'd like to see you once a week for a little while so that I can get over the silly moodiness of mine and stop being such a pest.[10]

Though it would be difficult to tell from this brief statement of presenting complaints, this patient turned out to be a highly imaginative, secretly creative individual. She had given up college and the beginning of a promising career in the arts in order to do what was expected of her. She worked at a better-paying but less interesting job to subsidize her husband's completing law school. Then she gave herself over completely to the wife/mother role, ready to settle for little more than being a good girl who would be rewarded for her innocence by being protected and taken care of.

She had been as good as can be and her husband had given her "everything a woman could possibly want." She and the children were symbols of *his* success. He displayed them in a gracious home in a prestigious neighborhood, dressed them fashionably, and uncomplainingly laid out vast sums of money for the special lessons and opportunities to which the family of a man in his position was entitled. He had bought my patient her very own town-and-country station wagon so that she might ferry the children to the riding, ballet, and music academies.

He had even persuaded her to take an expensive course in French cooking. Returning home early one afternoon from his successful law firm, again he found her in tears. This time, he did not blow up at her. Instead, hiding his irritation, he went right out and bought her a $200 Cuisinart, so that she might experience more luxuriously the creative joys of gourmet cooking. To his dismay, she screamed and cried even more unreasonably. In a fit of temper, she smashed his beautiful gift.

That was the final straw. He explained to her how crazy she had become. She was filled with guilt proportionate to the enormity of her ingratitude. Together they agreed that she must go to a shrink who would cure whatever the hell was wrong with her.

After listening quietly to this account of her "nervous breakdown," I invited her to tell me some things about herself that had nothing to do with her husband. The first thing she spoke of was her father's sudden, unexpected death when she was only three years old. Fortunately, her mother and her grandmother had been very supportive and sensible about the whole matter. Father's insurance had left them very well off. The family would "never have to worry about money or anything else." Gradually they convinced her that she was not to waste her time crying. Daddy was now happy living with God in heaven. Our Lord had chosen to take daddy early because He loved him so. The little girl was fortunate to have had so wonderful a daddy even if only for a little while. Daddy was watching over her from heaven and what he wanted most was for her to be a good little girl, to do everything she was supposed to do, and most of all to be perfectly happy.

Her father's death and the ways she had been "helped to accept it" seemed to constitute her entire vision of her life up to the beginning of her naïve account of her marriage. When I expressed an interest in her briefly mentioned adolescent efforts at writing poetry, she went on to reveal an inner world filled with rich and beautiful symbols, subtle feelings, and great sensitivity. All of these she discounted as "silly." Writing poetry was only a self-indulgence she had "fooled with" for a while instead of doing something worthwhile.

Offering my expert diagnosis of her problems, I told her that I believed that she was going sane! Psychotherapy was indicated in cases like hers because it helped in two ways. First, even short-term weekly meetings with a therapist could help her to become clearer about those aspects of her life that gave her sound reason to be unhappy. And if she would consider more intensive, long-term psychotherapy, she might even get a chance to accept her imperfections enough to make room for occasional irrational unhappiness.

If she wanted to limit her treatment to the first aid of the former approach, I would be glad to refer her to some other competent therapist who would be willing to help her that way. As for myself, I was only willing to get involved with her if she would meet with me at least twice (and perhaps later three times) a week for what might turn out to be a long time. If we could hang out together frequently and long enough to really get to know one another, then I would be happy to take her on as my patient.

She seemed thrown both by my diagnosis and by the terms of the treatment I offered. Still, she made the growth choice rather than the fear choice. We met again that week and continued to meet at least twice a week for almost three years.

Understandably, at first she found it very hard to trust me. She would present some "irrational" feeling of unhappiness with her marriage, hoping I would help her to overcome whatever flaw in herself had created this unwarranted discontent. Instead I would invite her curiosity about what in her marriage might give her good reason to be dissatisfied. During one such exchange, she became worried that *I* might be going crazy.

Her husband was generous and attentive. Still, in some ways she felt neglected and emotionally hungry. Didn't I understand that she was asking for more than she deserved?

I told her that it wasn't clear to me that anyone *deserved* anything. Sometimes we get what we want, sometimes we don't. Who knows who deserves and who doesn't?

Long ago I had given up trying to resolve such questions. I told her that attempting to find the answer to her question "What do I deserve?" seemed as useless to me as my own earlier efforts at deciding whether I was really a selfish or an unselfish person.

Even if it had been possible to discover the answer, I no longer believed that it could be of any conceivable use to me. I let her know that I was unhappy less often now that I had lost interest in such questions. If she hung out with me, I assured her that she too might lose an interest in make-believe problems of deserving and undeserving, selfish and unselfish, right and wrong, and good and bad.

Her "nervous breakdown" was simply an indication that her angelic posture no longer served as a fully successful denial of her darker side. If there was good and bad, she was both. Secretly she suffered from the painful effort needed to maintain her choice of living a life of doing what she should rather than doing as she pleased.

She tried to project the indulgent aspect onto me and then to struggle against it. When she accused me of being the Devil, I acknowledged always taking that role when faced with an Angel. Now that she had recognized me for what I was, I pointed out that she should flee this occasion of sin. If she stayed, I would take her remaining with me as tacit consent to my teaching her how to give in to temptation.

I made so much of how good she was and how bad I was that eventually she began to protest my outrageous exaggerations. Repeatedly, she would find herself arguing against my insisting that she was so different from anyone else. Often these "arguments" would end up with one of us breaking into laughter, and the other quickly giving way to the infectious release. These moments of abandon were warm and happy personal meetings.

After many months of therapy, she turned more seriously toward exploring the darker side of her self. She had come to feel safe and strong enough to begin to reveal her own secretly destructive impulses. It was a frightening threshold to cross.

It turned out that, unlike my earlier sweet murderers, she had killed no one. Still, she had more to confess than some terrible but unlived-out brutal fantasy. With deep shame, she told me how, as she put it, she had "made my little girl crazy." The little girl threatened to live out the self-indulgent abandon that my patient had so long ago learned to deny within herself. Telling herself that it was for the child's own good, the mother had set aside "a private time" each day during which she established and maintained a near-delusional fairy tale that the child had come to believe in.

I've gotten her to believe that I can see what she's doing any time of the day or night. She believes that I always know when she is doing something she shouldn't be doing. So she tries to be good all of the time. Whenever she has been bad she comes to me right away. She pleads with me to forgive her that time and promises never to do it again. I always forgive her, and she always ends up doing it again some time.

At first I thought I was helping her to be good, and keeping her from getting into trouble. Now I understand that all I've done is to make her crazy, and to keep her from enjoying doing as she pleases.

It's making me feel awful, and it's destroying her, but I just can't seem to stop.

Her anguished account revealed how right it had seemed when she instilled this fantasy in her little girl's head. But even when she realized she had turned the child's life into a mirror of her own tortured attempt to be perfect, she could not stop retelling the fairy tale that she and the child lived out each day.

Gradually during our time together, she was able to become less obsessed with guilt, confession, and seeking my forgiveness. As she lost interest in that compulsive litany, she became curious about how she had come to treat her child this way in the first place. The child's original innocence had served as a blank screen onto which she had projected her own wishes to break loose and risk getting into trouble. Once she was able to withdraw this projection, she was able to explore the disowned parts of herself, and to reevaluate their having been condemned.

Things have changed between my patient and her daughter, but it may take a long time to repair the damage done to this child. Like physical child-battering, unless the cycle is interrupted, emotional abuse of children is passed on from one generation to the next. Unlike literal homicide, this sort of soul murder is partially reversible. But it takes a long, long time, some scar tissue always remains, and some of us never fully recover.

Whether the damage done to themselves or others is physical or emotional, there is a high price to be paid for living the saintly life of heroic virtue. No human being is pure in thought, word, or action. We may be certain that anyone who appears to be angelic is too good to be true. Whatever an individual's conscious attitudes, the exact opposites exist in his or her unconscious. The more extreme and seemingly pure the conscious pose, the more energy it will take to contain its exactly equivalent counterpart and the greater danger that sometime unexpectedly the denied impulses may break loose in full savagery. Being on our own, each of us must take the personal responsibility of coming to know the wolf within or we risk becoming the lamb that slaughters the rest of the flock.

9

Someone to Look After Me

Our reluctance to accept being on our own is understandable. Learning that grown-ups have to take care of themselves is one of the more painful losses of innocence. As adults we can count on others to look after us in certain ways some of the time. Someone else may attend to our needs as an act of love or kindness, or simply because their services are for hire. It is unlikely, however, that our well-being can ever be as fundamentally important to anyone else as it is to ourselves.

Many personal and professional caretakers remain unconsciously focused on filling their own unmet needs for care. Some have become chronic helpers out of despair of ever finding someone to take care of them. Now when they feel hungry, they settle for feeding others.

In the process they often disregard the particular needs of the person who is being looked after. Consider the example of an affection-starved parent whose child complains about not understanding a homework assignment. Such parents are more likely to impose the sympathy that they themselves long to receive, than to offer the instruction that the child wants and needs.

Certainly some of the ways that people take care of one another are more useful and trustworthy than this. Caretaking can start out reliable, competent, and unselfishly attuned to the needs of those people who must depend on others doing what they cannot do for themselves.

But anyone who assumes a position of being responsible for another's care is subject to the corrupting temptations that come with that power. Even the most loving care soon is subtly transformed from offering what the dependent asks for to imposing what the donor believes the other person should have (for his or her own good). It is difficult to take responsibility for other people's well-being without beginning to believe that we know what is best for them. The very need for care seems to discredit their competence or even their right to live their own lives.

At those times when any of us feel helpless enough to depend on others for care, we ourselves may begin to believe that they know what is best for us, better than we do ourselves. Even when people who take care of one another do have each other's interests at heart, the best laid plans may go awry. These unforeseen costs in the reciprocal relationship of one person looking after another are the central motifs of John Steinbeck's prize-winning play-novelette, *Of Mice and Men*.[1]

The central characters are two symbiotic itinerant ranchworkers. Lennie is a big dumb ox of a man whose simple innocence is characterized metaphorically by his mental retardation. George, a sharp little smart-assed cynic, looks after the grateful Lennie. George describes how their interdependent bonding began:

One day a bunch of guys was standin' around up on the Sacramento River. I was feelin' pretty smart. I turns to Lennie and says, "Jump in." An' he jumps. Couldn't swim a stroke. He damn near drowned before we could get him. An' he was so damn nice to me for pullin' him out. Clean forgot I told him to jump in. Well, I ain't done nothing like that no more.[2]

Lennie is so grateful for being rescued that he ignores completely that it was George who almost got him drowned in the first place. Knowing that he cannot take care of himself, Lennie submits easily to any seemingly helpful adult who presumes to know what's best for him. This dumb, trusting submissiveness gives George power over him. Ironically, it also burdens George with the responsibility for looking after Lennie.

George complains that if he had no one else to worry about, he could be happy and free. But clearly if he did not have Lennie to take care of there would be no meaning to George's otherwise empty life. By catering to Lennie's innocence, there are moments when George himself can begin to believe that they will someday live happily ever after. Like a world-weary parent who finds con-

solation for personal hopelessness in the nightly retelling of a familiar bedtime story to a trusting child, George can sometimes find
hope for himself in the story he has made up to fulfill Lennie's
inarticulate yearnings for a happy ending.

And so wordlessly they have conspired to have Lennie pester
George into telling him "about the rabbits." Again and again,
George gives in reluctantly to retell the story they both love so well.
But it is Lennie who must seem to need looking after.

"Tell me—like you done before."

"Tell you what?"

"About the rabbits."

George snapped, "You ain't gonna put nothing over on me."

Lennie pleaded, "Come on, George. Tell me. Please, George. Like you
done before."

"You get a kick outta that, don't you? Awright, I'll tell you, and then
we'll eat our supper. . . ."

George's voice became deeper. He repeated his words rhythmically as
though he had said them many times before. "Guys like us, that work on
ranches, are the loneliest guys in the world. They got no family. They
don't belong no place. They come to a ranch an' work up a stake and
then they go inta town and blow their stake, and the first thing you know
they're poundin' their tail on some other ranch. They ain't got nothing to
look ahead to."

Lennie was delighted. "That's it—that's it. Now tell how it is with us."

George went on. "With us it ain't like that. We got a future. We got
somebody to talk to that gives a damn about us. We don't have to sit in
no bar room blowin' in our jack jus' because we got no place else to go.
If them other guys gets in jail they can rot for all anybody gives a damn.
But not us."

Lennie broke in. *"But not us! An' why? Because . . . because I got you
to look after me, and you got me to look after you, and that's why."* He
laughed delightedly. "Go on now, George!"

"You got it by heart. You can do it yourself."

"No, you. I forget some a' the things. Tell about how it's gonna be."

"O.K. Someday—we're gonna get the jack together and we're gonna
have a little house and a couple of acres an' a cow and some pigs and—"

"An' live off the fatta the lan'," Lennie shouted. "An' have *rabbits*.
Go on, George! Tell about what we're gonna have in the garden and
about the rabbits in the cages and about the rain in the winter and the
stove, and how thick the cream is on the milk like you can hardly cut it.
Tell about that, George."

"Why'n't you do it yourself? You know all of it."

"No . . . you tell it. It ain't the same if I tell it. Go on . . . George. How I get to tend the rabbits."

"Well," said George, "we'll have a big vegetable patch and a rabbit hutch and chickens. And when it rains in the winter, we'll just say the hell with goin' to work, and we'll build up a fire in the stove and set around it an' listen to the rain comin' down on the roof. . . ." [3]

And George goes on to tell the rest of the story, with Lennie making sure none of the good parts are left out. By now it's difficult to know which of these innocents is being looked after.

Inevitably their plans end in futility and defeat. Innocently Lennie gets into trouble. Without meaning any harm, trying only to protect his dream about the rabbits, he murders a woman who threatens the dream's coming true. In turn, as a final act of looking after Lennie, George decides that shooting Lennie will be better for him than allowing him to face the consequences of his act. To avoid the loss of innocence, Lennie has killed a stranger, and George has killed a friend.

To preserve their pseudo-innocent dreams of life as it should be, George and Lennie destroy any prospects of what they might have had. Many of the unhappy people who come to me for psychotherapy have also sacrificed whatever they might have found in life as it is.

It has always started out sensibly enough. As children they grew up in families that treated them so badly that accepting life as it was became intolerable. Without the protection of pseudo-innocent illusions they would have died of despair. There was little recourse but to overcome their helplessness by creating some life-enhancing fantasy in which to believe.

At the time, the original belief in these childhood illusions served as a useful solution to an otherwise desperately hopeless situation. These people have long since grown beyond having to be dependent on the families that did not treat them well. Still they cling to pseudo-innocent belief in personal fairy tales. Continuing to believe in illusions that once served to free them from what was an intolerable present now traps them in a chronically anguished past. Beliefs that once served as solutions have now been transformed into problems. If these patients are to grow beyond their neurotically unhappy lives, psychotherapy must offer the opportunity for a further loss of innocence.

For some the pseudo-innocence takes the form of a life-long search for a magic way to make people care about them. If only they could learn to enchant others with their grace and beauty, to please them with their compliance, impress them with their achievements, or manipulate them with their wiles, then they could live happily ever after. At last they would be safe, looked after, and maybe even loved.

For others the solution lies in finding some way to vindicate themselves. Justice must triumph. Some day the victims will be rescued and the oppressors punished. Bad parents would then feel regret at having mistreated them and make up for past neglect. Some neurotics waste their lives in search for the good parents they once so desperately needed but never had. Surely fate must compensate them for early deprivations.

Some would settle for little more than an explanation for their unhappiness. It all would seem bearable, perhaps even worthwhile, if only somehow they could make sense of their suffering. They try making up reasons to account for their unhappy childhoods but are never quite satisfied with their own explanations. Surely someone somewhere must know the answer. They undertake a lifelong search for someone wiser than themselves.

If only they could attach themselves to someone who knew the true meaning of life, that magic helper could be depended upon to look after them. Unfortunately the reciprocally neurotic caretaker is not so hard to find. But anyone willing to do the caretaking may demand that the dependent one become exactly what is needed to complete the casting of the helper's own fairy tale. Usually both end up disappointed.

Stubbornly insisting on trusting other people's judgments instead of their own, again and again the dependent seekers find themselves let down, exploited, and betrayed. Still the search goes on for someone who is sufficiently wise and kind to be trusted with responsibility for their well-being. The prospect of repeated disappointments is awful. But giving up the hope of being looked after poses the overwhelming prospect of being on one's own.

Such people can hardly bear even imagining what it would be like to recognize that they are in charge of their own lives. When I suggest to them that then they would be free to do as they please, they seem terrified. Claiming that they do not really know what they want, they seem sure that making their own decisions would mess up their lives.

Sometimes I point out that the patient's dependence on others has already made a mess out of his or her life. "That may be true," the patient concurs reluctantly, "but it's not my fault that the people I've counted on always turn out to be as uncaring as my mother (or father). In any case, I have no choice. I was never properly cared for when I was young, so how can I be expected to take care of myself now? I know that I'm almost twenty-five (or thirty-five, or forty-five) years old, but inside I'm still a little boy (or girl). I don't know how to take care of myself. Besides it's not fair that I should have to."

A woman suffering from this petulant style of pseudo-innocence recently sought my help for chronic smiling depression. There was no trace of anguish in her insistently hopeful tone of voice as she recounted her many disappointments. She described her situation simply and clearly: "I have put myself in the hands of many Masters. It has turned out that none of them really knew the true meaning of life. I tried everything that they told me to do, but nothing helped for very long. I am still unhappy. My life is still not wonderful. I've read your books. They did help a little. So now I have come to sit at your feet so that you may teach me the true answer, the one I need to solve all my problems."

Years ago, when I first encountered this style of pseudo-innocence, I was put off by what seemed a put-on. I did not then understand that these people were trying to fool not me, but themselves. Back then I dismissed such people summarily. They did not seem to take psychotherapy seriously enough to warrant my accepting them as patients.

Now I understand that what I experienced as intentional petulance was beyond their conscious control. These people contributed to my misunderstanding them by pretending aloud that their compulsively demanding attitudes were freely chosen. Most of their adult lives had been spent in the degradation of misleadingly presenting themselves as overgrown toddlers who deliberately pouted and tantrumed just to get their own way. Better to pretend that they were in charge of such childish self-mockery than to face being grown-ups helpless to do anything about having to live uncompensated lives, forever cheated out of getting a cared-for childhood.

Now that I understand the profound desperation behind their seemingly shallow self-indulgence, I am no longer willing to dismiss such people without a hearing. They try to elevate me to the position of seer and savior. I let them know that I haven't had much luck in finding answers that would make me or anyone else able to live happily ever after. Instead I offer the possibility that we could spend some time together and see if we enjoy getting to know one another. This invitation usually evokes a history of the disappointing predecessors whose help had already failed.

If the particular patient I began to describe earlier had known of a newly forming Guru-of-the-Month Club, she would have signed up as a charter member. I was to be no more than the most recent candidate for failure in the long line of flawed magic helpers left in the wake of her disappointing passage. Every new person in her life might be the one she sought.

During the past ten years, she had actively transferred responsibility for management of her life from one professional caretaker to another. First she had turned to the family lawyer, then to the local minister. After that she was let down by a university counselor, and most recently by a transactional-analysis group leader. I was her last hope.

According to her account, each of my predecessors had tried to meet her demand that he show her the way. She was a quick study. In each setting she had learned to walk the walk and to talk the talk demanded by the theatrical traditions of the particular helping profession whose wise counsel she had sought. Each time that she converted to a new way of life, the respective magic helper would confirm her as elevated to the rank of "sensible," "saved," "mature," or "game-free" (depending on his designation for "cured").

For a time, each helper had maintained the professional posture of insisting that she take responsibility for her own life. In response to the power of her petulant helplessness, each was soon manipulated into agreeing that she was too fragile and childlike to know what was best for her. One after another, these consultants were seduced into the role of savior.

Briefly, the patient would feel "wonderful" about being so special as to have got her own way. Paradoxically, each time she was able to get one of these men to take over by telling her how to run her life, she would soon end up feeling contempt for his yielding, and disdain for his "dumb answers." Finally she would fire the most recent helper and go off in search of someone else who could provide better magic. Ever hopeful, she went on being unhappy, burdened by the needless suffering of repeated disappointments. Stubbornly she insisted that there must be someone somewhere who would look after her in a way that would make her life wonderful.

It was understandable that she was hungry for someone to look after her. As one of the youngest children in a large, underprivileged, rural Southern family she received little more than crowded room and meager board, paternal beatings and maternal neglect.

Overwhelmed by their own childhood deprivations and the frustration of feeling trapped in the powerless confines of ignorance and poverty, her parents experienced each child as yet another unwanted burden unfairly imposed on their already weary backs. Humiliated and enraged by his inability to support his family decently, father often got drunk and beat up his wife and kids. Afterward he felt even worse about himself. This usually spiraled into another round of despair, drinking, and violence.

How vividly my patient remembered the few brief interludes when her father had seemed kinder. These were times when he had joined some group that he hoped would change his life. But none of his immersions in the Baptist Church, the Freemasons, and the Klan ever lasted very long. He could go from skeptic, to convert, to defector in a matter of weeks. And then hard times and hopelessness would be back, worse than ever it seemed.

Wandering off in the solace of her own wishful fantasies, mother gave no more to my patient than father did. In the midst of the barrenness and brutality that was her world, mother maintained herself on the reassuring fiction of the wonderful life she could have had if only she had not married so early, if only she had chosen a more promising mate, if only she had not had so many children so fast, etc. But for this, and but for that, surely she could have/would have been a star.

From the time mother was a little girl, she had had that special something. Lots of people told her so. She even had been on the stage, and not just in public school plays. Some folks said she was the prettiest, most talented young teen-ager who had ever sung and danced in the county-theater group.

How she longed to be discovered, to be catapulted to stardom, to Broadway, maybe even to Hollywood. But there had been no one to show her the way.

Mother had made the mistake of attaching herself to the first strong young man who showed a serious interest in her. Hoping that he would look after her, she let him make the decisions, first about when they would marry, and later about when they would have children. When they were courting, he had seemed really excited about how someday she could make it big in show business. Later on, he wouldn't even listen to her. By then all she wanted was a chance to dream aloud about all that had been lost. He told her there was no time to dream what with all the children and never enough cash. Besides it was crazy to think that people like them could ever amount to anything special.

She should have run off to New York or to Hollywood while she had had the chance. Now it was too late. If only someone had discovered her, recognized how special she could have become, they could have shown her how to become a star. But she'd never found anyone to look after her career that way. Again and again she would complain to the kids about how instead she had made the mistake of listening to their father.

During the first few weeks of therapy my patient echoed her own updated version of mother's lament. She too had not yet found that special someone who would show her how to attain that wonderful life her future must yet hold in store. Just from reading my books, she could tell that I "really had it together." Now that she'd met me she could see that I was just the sort of counselor she had been seeking. The others had turned out to be duds, but she was sure that I would not fail her. If only I would instruct her, she was absolutely certain that she could fulfill her extraordinary potential.

The focus of our early work was centered on her longing to be taken care of. Mostly I reflected back her feelings in a way that would allow her to experience the anguished vulnerability and poignant sadness that underlay her willfully insistent wish for happily-ever-aftering.

Gradually my emphasis shifted to heightening awareness of her self-defeating pseudo-innocent lifestyle. As trust in our therapeutic alliance grew, she began to feel safe enough to become more and more conscious of what she was doing, of how she was doing it, and eventually of why she was living out this wishful fantasy.

It was painfully difficult for her to begin to accept her adult life as it was. Each time she faced clearly yet another hidden aspect of her insistence that someone must look after her, she would experience some more of the anguish and the vulnerability of having to live the rest of her life without compensation for having missed the loving care so desperately needed when she was a child.

The core reactions to that deprivation were rage, grief, and helplessness. These had to be faced, a bit at a time, as she felt ready for each new disclosure. Tortured episodes of recognition and release were always followed by the interludes of rest and withdrawal that she needed to begin to integrate each new disclosure. The spiraling course of her reentry and retreat deepened with each new sweep of expanding consciousness.

There was a hidden context for her apparent relinquishing of the hope that someone would look after her. On the edge of her awareness was the belief that if she accepted her despair like a good girl then I would reward her efforts. If she could just be my very best patient then in the end I would yield and accept responsibility for her well-being.

We were well into our second year of her psychotherapy when the emptiness of this last desperate illusion became clear. She had spent the first part of the session reviewing the marvelous "progress" made during her time in treatment with me. She had left her long-unhappy marriage. Her dead-end secretarial job had been relinquished for a position with professional-level career options. No longer preoccupied with what others thought of her, she was far freer to do as she pleased.

The second half of the session was devoted to a poignant account of the new problems engendered by all this progress. No longer tied to a reliably oppressive husband, she had to negotiate relationships with less consistent men. The new job involved administrative responsibilities that she had never before been allowed. Faced with more energy and less mess, she felt overwhelmed at the prospect of being free to decide what to do with her life. She detailed the many situational decisions that *I* must now help her to make. Having remained largely silent up to that point, I finally responded sympathetically: "It's hard being all grown up."

She nodded vigorously in agreement, paused for a deep sigh, and then went on to detail the many new choices open to her. She found it all just too hard to decide on her own. My continued silence prompted her to plead, "I've come as far as I can on my own and it hasn't been easy. Now I'm faced with decisions I've never had to make before. You've got to tell me what to do."

For the remainder of the hour she met my continuing silence with her own. Just as our time was about up, she found words for her exasperation: "You're not giving me the answers again today. I've done everything you've expected of me as a patient, but still you won't tell me what to do. You act like you really don't care what I do with my life, that it's all up to me. Sometimes it feels like you're no help at all. Why am I paying you all this money?"

She paused for a moment, her attention caught by some inner vision that interrupted her petulant stream of complaints. Her eyes widened in the wonder that comes with the sudden realization of an insight so simple that it may be overlooked for a lifetime. Her voice had the exaggerated deliberateness of someone who can hardly believe what she is saying: "Do you mean to tell me that this is all there is to it? I spend thirty years trying to find someone to look after me, and *this* is what I end up with? It's taken me all this time to find out that I have to pay fifty dollars an hour to get someone who will listen to my troubles *without* telling me how to run my life!"

I have more than enough trouble looking after myself. It's hard enough deciding how to run my own life without trying to figure out what's best for someone else.

As a psychotherapist, I am committed to offering my expert

technical services in helping my patients become more conscious of how they do run their lives. In that way they may come to understand what they get out of living as they do, and at what costs. My assistance in this guided self-examination is likely to increase their awareness of options, but at my best I understand that their actual choosing is none of my business.

We all do well to hear about other people's experiences with situations similar to those we face. Even their opinions may be usefully considered. In some instances, hiring expert consultants turns out to be helpful. But after gathering information, opinions, and technical services, we end up still faced with whether or not we will follow whatever advice has been garnered.

The proportion of responsibility that we delegate may depend on what sort of problem is to be solved. It is one thing to pay a plasterer to judge whether the dining-room ceiling should be patched up or torn down. Problems at the plasterer's end of the spectrum are trivial compared with those that require our hiring a divorce lawyer. Like the plasterer, the attorney may be needed to give technical assistance and advice. Some measure of trust is required even in letting someone else decide whether a ceiling should be patched up or torn down. But what about problems of far greater personal importance? Anyone might delegate responsibility for deciding whether or not to try to patch up a crumbling ceiling. Only a pseudo-innocent would accept someone else looking after a crumbling marriage.

By the time I reached my thirties, much of the time I felt very much in charge of the personal decisions in my life. Like everyone else, at times I longed so for someone to look after me that I would let someone else make my decisions for me. The price always turned out to be too high, so I usually took care of business myself. I made many mistakes, but often enough things worked out well. I felt confident that no one else was better qualified than I to run my life.

For a while during the early part of my illness, I was able to maintain this clarity. I had long respected some physicians as competent practitioners of their folk art: the maintenance and repair of body plumbing. Still, I understood that medical experts sometimes disagreed, often erred, and rarely admitted that they did not know what was wrong.

I was no more awed by the authority of physicians than of other experts who would presume to tell me how to live. It was easy to sympathize with Virginia Woolf's account of what happened when her fictional hero/heroine Orlando, sought treatment for his/her symptom of having been asleep for a week:

... the doctors were hardly wiser than they are now, and after prescribing rest and exercise, starvation and nourishment, society and solitude, that he should lie in bed all day and ride forty miles between lunch and dinner, together with the usual sedatives and irritants, diversified, as the fancy took them, with possets of newt's slobber on rising, and draughts of peacock's gall on going to bed, they left him to himself, and gave it as their opinion that he had been asleep for a week.[4]

Ms. Woolf's description of medicine's magic helpers was written forty years prior to my illness. Back then no one consulted a physician except to be relieved of pain or cured of illness. By the time I was grown, it seemed almost natural that doctors looked after more and more aspects of our lives. The province of medical profession had been expanded from the treatment of illness to the expropriation of health.[5]

Supported more and more widely by legal sanctions, "medical science" has become the regulating social agency for seeing us through what were once the natural life cycles of birth, childhood, mating, pregnancy, aging, and death. When illness strikes we all experience the inevitable regression to childlike dependency. Government-supported medical supervision of our health simply encouraged our giving over responsibilities to physicians for decisions that are more personal than medical. During these last few years of illness, once more my survival has depended on my being able to give up being looked after. Some of the physicians who have diagnosed and treated my illness have been helpful. Some have not. In any case, it is *I* who must retain the power and responsibility for the personal decisions that these medical caretakers would otherwise make for me.

My first symptom appeared nine years ago. At first I thought that my telephone was intermittently out of order. Within a few days I had figured out that the problem was that I could no longer hear with my left ear. The family doctor was reassuring as he applied conservative treatments to try to remove ear wax, clear my sinus passages, etc.

When nothing worked, he sent me to an ear/nose/throat specialist. Trusting that this sweet little man was as wise as he was old, I agreed to meet with him for a series of "exploratory sessions." I underwent a wide spectrum of diagnostic tests and unsuccessful attempts at treatment. It seemed that nothing could break the spell. After several weeks he announced that he had successfully diagnosed my case. He told me that I was suffering the effects of a rare virus that has been known to strike men of my age. It comes without warning, resulting in an overnight loss of hearing in one ear. Fortunately, there are no other symptoms. Unfortunately, neither is there a cure.

He reassured me that there was no danger of my other ear becoming involved, but also told me that the condition was irreversible. I was to adjust to the hearing loss as best I could. It was a bad break but no further medical attention was required.

Despite his reassurances, I was terrified by the possibility of becoming personally isolated by total deafness. This fear encouraged my challenging his expert advice. I told him that I wanted a second opinion, but I made the mistake of asking him to choose a consultant for me. He referred me to another ear specialist, who in turn made the same *mis*diagnosis. In any case, though I did not believe that "doctors know best," I was sufficiently intimidated by their expert consensus to yield to their "wisdom."

I learned to live with my loss. At first I found myself withdrawing from situations in which I had trouble hearing clearly. Hearing with only one ear makes localization of sound very difficult. As a consequence, in a group it was hard for me to know who was speaking unless I saw them speak. Open-space situations like restaurants were particularly confusing. I was unable to sort out what was being said at my table and what part of what I was hearing was simply background noise from other diners. But with some help from my friends and family I began to be careful to sit in the most advantageous locations, to let people know when I wasn't sure who had spoken, and to tell any new person that I met that I was deaf in one ear and that I would appreciate his or her speaking up.

As with all handicaps, a partial hearing loss even had its advantages. It did not take long for me unwittingly to transform this loss into an adaptive screening device. Once I had more limited access to sound, it soon became apparent that it was easier for me to hear kind words than to hear criticism. As the months went by, I grew less and less preoccupied with this isolated auditory symptom.

A year later, I developed vertigo. Whenever I turned my head I experienced an awful sense of dizziness as if the world was spinning about all around me. This time I didn't bother seeing the family physician, but went directly to a well-recommended internist. He was aware of my hearing loss but did not connect it with the vertigo. My second symptom resulted in a second *mis*diagnosis. This time I was told I had a mild middle-ear infection. These conditions were difficult to treat, but not to worry, they tended to run their course and clear up without medical intervention.

Already stuck with the hearing loss, this time I was determined to take the best possible care of myself. I told the internist that despite his advice I would seek further consultation. I refused his referral to a friendly colleague who might unwittingly offer a less than objective evaluation. Instead I researched the problem until I believed I had identified the best teaching hospital in the area. In that way I was most likely to have a team of well-trained, up-to-date senior specialists checking out each other's contribution to my medical care.

Insisting that *I* had to decide what was best for me, I overrode the internist's judgment and saved my life. Allowing the first two hearing specialists to decide *for me* may have foreshortened it. The combined evaluations of the training hospital's ear/nose/throat and neurological departments resulted in the first correct diagnosis: acoustic neuroma, a nonmalignant brain tumor situated on the left auditory nerve. The tumor had caused both the hearing loss and the vertigo. Unless it was removed surgically, it would cause more and more damage as it continued to grow. Gratuitously, I was assured that the first physicians' errors were understandable. It seems that such tumors are often misdiagnosed in their earliest stages.

There was some danger in my undergoing the surgery, but the tumor was probably still small enough to be removed safely and completely. Of the five hospitals in America purported to have the best specialized neurosurgical teams, the closest was Massachusetts General Hospital in Boston.

Despite reassurances by the diagnostic center's doctors, I was terribly frightened that I would die. My family and I thought of little else during the weeks of waiting for the scheduled surgery. We talked about our fears, comforted each other and upset each other. We alternated being realistic with pretending there was nothing really to worry about. We went through all the approaches and avoidances that people attempt when facing an overwhelmingly frightening, ultimately unmanageable personal situation.

The surgery was to be a two-stage procedure. First I was to undergo a "simple" entry just behind my left ear. When I had recovered from this operation, the neurosurgical team would attempt to remove the remainder of the tumor with a second entry through the base of my skull. They hoped that in this way, risk of extensive neurological damage would be minimized.

By the time I flew up to Boston for the operation, I had recovered some of my bravado. The section of Massachusetts General in which the ear surgery was to be conducted was just right for my more familiar maverick posture:

an old-timey, nursing-staff-dominated hospital cluttered with arbitrary rules, allegedly for the patients' benefit but clearly to make things easier on the staff. Especially during the preoperative days of further diagnostic testing, this afforded me just the sort of challenge I needed to assert the impact of my personal identity as a way of escaping . . . how scared and helpless I felt.[6]

The first night I was assigned to a room housing two other patients. One of them was an old man who obviously was dying. He moaned tormentedly as he awaited that release. Having to listen to him put me back in touch with my own terror. I went to the head floor-nurse to tell her how upsetting it was to hear the old man's pain, and how it kept me preoccupied with the fear that I too would die. I wanted to have my room changed. She explained to me that everything was all right, that of course the old man was *not* dying (he died the next night), and that I had nothing to worry about. (*I* lived the next day but went on worrying.)

One of the nurse's functions in the hospital subculture is the denial of trouble. While her stated intent is to make the patient feel better, much of this seems to be done for the convenience of an efficiently run hospital. Worried patients are a bother. They demand individual personal attention and they question the staff's case management of them.

As soon as the nurse left, I sneaked out and down the hall until I found a room with an unassigned bed. Returning to my original room, I gathered up my belongings and took them to my new room. I made sure to shift my name tags from one bed and door to the other so that I wouldn't get someone else's operation.

The next morning the nursing staff was in an uproar. They were in charge. That was the message. They knew best. They would take care of me if only I would keep my mouth shut. One of the effects of the hospital subculture's defining itself as in charge and taking care of everything is that patients become interchangeable units. They deal with the patients in dehumanizing ways that deny his or her feelings. This can even result in errors in which one patient, no different from the other except for his or her name tag, may be given the wrong medication, etc.

Taking this into account, one friend chose to break through for me. That first night I heard a call on the intercom loudspeaker asking that Dr. Kopp come to the phone. I got out of bed and went to the nursing station and announced that I was Dr. Kopp. Because I wore a bathrobe and a hospital gown that opened up to expose my ass, they told me that I could not possibly be a doctor. I must be just a patient. I insisted that I was both a patient and a doctor, that indeed the call was for me, and that I damn well would take it. When I picked up the phone my friend in Washington said: "Hey, man, I just want to let them know that we can get through to you whenever you need us." I hid my tears from the nurse.

The first operation went well and I was able to return home for a two-week recuperation before returning for the second and more formidable ordeal. I had underestimated the enormous physical and emotional impact that even the simplest major surgery would have. Though still insistent that I was an indomitable survivor, I found my usually spirited self-reliance yielding to increased longings to be looked after. Talking with the neurosurgeon on the evening before the second operation, I found myself pulled back and forth between these seemingly contradictory wishes.

This man is the consummate neurosurgeon. He is a highly skilled technician, a master craftsman. He has the emotional detachment it takes to spend twelve hours operating on another human being's brain. But in his own detached way, he is considerate of his patients as people and makes sure that he is available to give straightforward answers to any medical questions they might wish to raise.

That night he was explaining to me what the chances were of my surviving the operation and describing the residual handicaps that might constitute the cost of that survival. There were many dangers including weakness, disfigurement, and paralysis. During his detailed account of these outcomes, he noticed that I was crying. It is the only time I have seen him even begin to look upset. "Pull yourself together, Dr. Kopp," he remonstrated.

"I'm the most together patient you're ever going to operate on," I protested. "You've just been telling me that by tomorrow I may be dead or crippled. If someone was telling you awful things about your future, you'd be crying too."

"I suppose that's normal under the circumstances," he mumbled before going on with his answers to my questions.

The operation turned out to be a partial success. Most of the tumor was removed. At that time it was not yet clear whether the sliver left on my brainstem would slough off or grow again. Still I had survived. My vertigo had been reduced to mild imbalance. Added to the irreversible partial deafness, there were daily headaches to be endured. But it could have been much worse. Once past the seemingly unbearable postoperative pain and the brief psychotic reaction, I felt happy to be alive and grateful to the doctors. It was several months before I crashed emotionally. All the depression I had been denying surged up to fill the vacation-vulnerable space of weeks without my work as a protective distraction. After a suicidal summer I returned to psychotherapy as a patient once more. I needed to sort out the changes in my life. It would have been hard for anyone to make sense of the experiences I had endured. The pain of my own struggle was exaggerated by the attendant shattering of my pseudo-innocent beliefs. I had been the rugged individualist, the avenging sword of justice, the mother of outcasts. None of that mattered. Some people get their lives shortened by tumors. Some do not. What happened happened, and there was much of it that was beyond even understanding, much less controlling. If there was any worth left in trying to live life as a just man, it had to be done in an unjust world. There was no appeal, no one to blame. It was go on and kill yourself, or get on with it.

Three years after the first set of operations, I developed a new symptom. By the middle of the afternoon each day I was wiped out by overwhelming fatigue. When I returned to Boston for an evaluation, I was told that the tumor had grown again and further surgery would be required.

Without questioning the advice of the neurologist and the surgeon, I underwent a second twelve-hour operation. Again the tumor could not be completely removed. It had become too deeply embedded in my brainstem. I was told that the tumor would continue to grow, that it would require further surgery every two to five years, and that eventually I would die in surgery. Each time I survived an operation I could expect to suffer some further handicap.

Mass. General is referred to as the Mecca of neurosurgery. These physicians had saved my life twice. For a while I was sure that they knew best how to look after me. I resumed the running of the rest of my life, but the medical aspects I turned over to them. Many people suggested I consider other kinds of help. Some urged me to turn to prayer, some to psychic healing, to all kinds of cures both wacky and sane. The only thing on which they all agreed was that I should not depend too much on the doctors.

I insisted that I already had the finest medical help available in the whole country, perhaps in the whole world. Twice my doctors had saved my life. Surely they were the ones meant to look after me. Part of this unshakable faith still makes good sense to me. Part of it was no more than my insistence that at last I had found someone who knew what was best for me.

In May 1976, three years after my second round of neurosurgery, I underwent a prescheduled monitoring of my condition. It was not that I had any new complaints. My doctors had instructed me to return to Boston semiannually so that any further tumor growth could be evaluated. Dutifully, I followed the doctors' orders without question.

I had no new symptoms. The neurologist's examination revealed no new signs. This time it was the machines that got me. The computerized brain scan is one of medical science's most advanced pieces of technology. Replacing the painful, dangerous diagnostic procedures I had undergone earlier, this machine takes several series of cross-sectional skull x-rays, processes them through the monitoring computer, and accurately evaluates previously mercurial soft-tissue changes.

After completing his examination, the neurologist told me that my condition seemed stable. He had found no evidence of new tumor growth. It was very likely that the brain-scan findings would confirm his own. The report of those results would be available in about a week. He would have his secretary contact me at that time.

Like my neurosurgeon, this neurologist is an acknowledged expert in his field of specialization. Less personally straightforward than the surgeon, he is sometimes patronizing in deciding what is best for me. Examples range from his euphemistically referring to my operations as "decompressions" to his dismissing my postoperative headache pain as "irrelevant." By "irrelevant" he means that my pain would be of interest only if it contributed to the differential diagnosis. He gives me the feeling that he treats tumors, not patients.

Soon he wrote to tell me that unexpectedly the computer findings indicated the recurrence of tumor growth resulting in further displacement of the brain. Remembering my having expressed concern about "deficits produced by surgery," he did not want to press me. Still, the computer findings did indicate that I should have another operation very soon.

Suddenly it all became chillingly clear. Up till then, I had believed that this magic helper knew what was best for me. All the while, he had looked to the computer as his own magic helper, one that knew what was best for him to do. It was time to take back the power I had trustingly given over to the doctors.

The shattering of my naïve attachment to these caretakers freed my attention for revaluation of my own priorities. So many of my personal concerns had come to depend on their medical interventions. Yet another operation might leave me further handicapped, perhaps even dead. At the very least it would mean more pain and terror. My own life and those of the people who love me would be turned upside down for weeks, as they had twice before in the last six years.

All of these personal issues now felt more important than what the computer had told the doctor. The computer had said that I was so impaired that I must set aside all of these other concerns to give medical technology authority over my life. But now the bottom line for me was that I was not hurting. Caretakers be damned! I decided that this time I would look after my self.

I spoke to my wife about my unwillingness to give myself over even to these trusted doctors at a time when I experienced no direct personal need for surgery. As always she let me know that I could count on her being there to support me in any decision I made. It was up to me to choose. Before I did, she hoped I would call the neurosurgeon and get more information from him.

Gratefully I accepted her support and trusted her counsel. I called the surgeon to ask two questions: If I chose to delay the surgery until it was needed to relieve distress from the new symptoms that must inevitably appear, would the delay affect my chance of surviving? Would it increase the probability of my being further handicapped?

With usual clarity and candor, the surgeon calmly informed me that my chances of survival would not be affected by the delay. These risks were the same every time I underwent surgery. However, he went on to point out that, as I knew from painful personal experience, surgery could not always reverse symptoms once they had appeared. As a result, if I chose to delay surgery, I increased the probability of postoperative handicaps.

I thanked him for the directness of his response, thought it over for a few days, and let him know that I had chosen to delay surgery until I felt the need for it. I made it clear to him that the recommendation for surgery in the absence of new symptoms had led me to rethink my entire situation. I now understood that it was entirely up to me to separate out the personal from the medical aspects of my decision. We agreed that I should return late that fall for further evaluation. The whole matter could be reconsidered at that time.

I felt both relieved and scared to be temporarily free of their looking after me. But before I was to return to Boston for the next scheduled neurological examination, unexpectedly I suffered a major heart attack. Had I undergone the previously recommended surgery, I surely would have died on the operating table.

Suddenly all bets were off. I had made a strong recovery, but it was clear that I was just as likely to be killed by my heart condition as I was by my brain tumor. After the initial recovery period there were occasional chest pains. I consulted the physician who had seen me through the heart attack. He told me that unless these symptoms responded in certain predictable ways, *he* might be faced with a very grave decision. I questioned how any grave decision to be made in this context would be his rather than mine. He explained that he might have to use a diagnostic procedure he preferred to avoid. When he named it, I asked if that wasn't the test that involved inserting a needle into the patient's heart, and didn't half of the patients die as a result of these tests. He assured me that though the test was risky, I had an exaggerated idea of how many patients died. It was fewer than I imagined, though still enough for this to remain a difficult decision for a doctor to have to make.

I couldn't believe what I was hearing from this otherwise decent, intelligent man. Supposing *he* decided that I must undergo this test, and just suppose I survived it, how would the test have helped me? I asked. The doctor explained that the results of the test would serve as a guide for a coronary bypass, simple heart surgery that would replace my insufficient artery with an improved plastic valve. By now the doctor was so immersed in translating these complex medical matters into terms that even a patient could understand that he could not hear my sardonic tone.

"And if I'm lucky enough to survive the diagnostic test, and then if the bypass works just right, Doctor, what would all that do for me?" I asked. Without missing a stroke, he replied brightly, "That would allow you to survive future brain surgery without having to worry about your heart giving out during the next operation."

At just that moment, still another piece of my innocence fell away. I had listened to how they would look after me and I realized how easily I might die of such caretaking. I assured the doctor *he* had nothing more to worry about. From now on I would only hire doctors to advise me, but never again to decide for me. I would have to consider even their best technical advice within the priorities of my nonmedical personal needs as I once again reclaimed full responsibility for running my life.

A few months later my resolve was put to the test. The doctors that looked after me in Boston wrote to tell me that they had scheduled another neurological examination and brain scan for me. I felt frightened that even a routine return to their territory would be sufficiently intimidating to undermine my determination to take care of myself. When I'm scared and uncertain, I'm most vulnerable to believing that someone somewhere must be smart enough to know what's best for me and strong enough to take care of me. When my anxiety is centered on my illness and the setting is authoritatively medical, the combination is hard to resist. It would be so tempting to cry out, "Doctor/Mommy/Daddy, I promise I'll be good from now on. Just take care of me. I'll do whatever you tell me."

I told my wife that I was determined not to undergo any further surgery until I felt I needed it. I didn't want to have this test. Until I was in pain I didn't want to risk going anywhere near the hospital. Again she offered her full loyalty and again she urged me to get all the information I needed to be sure of my decision. My letter to the neurosurgeon read:

I am writing to solicit your opinion about the next step in my medical/personal odyssey.

Last May, in the absence of new symptoms, and without any changes showing up in my neurological examination, my brain scan showed evidence of further growth of my acoustic neuroma. Dr. A [the neurologist] recommended surgery at that time. My contacting you proved to be very helpful in making the decision I faced.

In response to my enquiries, you informed me that postponing the surgical intervention would not affect my chances of surviving the operation. You went on to point out that if I delayed surgery until new symptoms developed, I would risk being stuck with all or part of those symptoms.

As you know, I decided against undergoing surgery at that time. You may also be aware that I suffered a serious coronary occlusion in September. My cardiologist advised me that any major surgery within six months of the heart attack would be very dangerous. He sent a report to Dr. A to that effect. Recently I received a note from Dr. A's secretary scheduling me for a brain scan and a neurological in May of 1977.

As you can imagine, two bouts of neurosurgery plus a heart attack within seven years have constituted a considerable financial drain for me and for my family (as well as an incredible emotional burden). If I come to Boston for this scheduled brain scan the loss of income, travel expenses, and medical costs will amount to over $500. You will understand that I do not wish to suffer the costs of this examination unless it serves some real advantage to me.

If the results of this proposed examination will offer no clearer a picture than the one I confronted last year, there seems no point in undergoing it. I remain free of new symptoms. The condition of my heart remains uncertain. All other things being equal, delaying major surgery seems even wiser to me now than it did last spring. Be assured that when new symptoms appear, I am committed to returning for further surgery.

In light of all this, I would appreciate your advising me about any concrete advantages to *the living of my life* that would be offered by my coming up to Boston for another examination in the spring.

Ten days later, I received his reply:

Thank you for your letter of February 7, 1977. I understand your situation and agree that under the circumstances the best course to follow at the present time is to continue your life as you now are leading it and when new symptoms appear we will be happy to see you here in Boston.

Via a copy of this letter, I will let Dr. A know that the examination scheduled in May, 1977 should be cancelled.

With best regards.

So that's where it stands for me right now. I have a brain tumor and I have a heart condition. I'm going to go on hiring doctors to help me, and I'm going to go on firing them when they don't. I'm on my own and I'm the only one who can be trusted to decide what's best for me.

I wrote to my neurosurgeon to demand the return of full responsibility for the way I live my life. He wrote back to say, "Fine, you've got it." There remains a part of me that wishes he had told me that because of the tumor I no longer knew what was best for me. That pseudo-innocent part of me longs for his assurance that I need not worry because I have him to look after me. I understand that this longing is a temptation against which I must continue to struggle every day for the rest of my life.

PART THREE

DEALING
WITH
DISENCHANTMENT

Come away, O human child!
To the waters and the wild
With a faery, hand in hand,
For the world's more full of weeping
    than you can understand.
                    William Butler Yeats,
                    "The Stolen Child"

10

Communal Innocence

Compared with other species of animals, human beings endure the longest period of helpless infancy and the slowest development to full maturity. Additionally burdened by evolved consciousness, children face a risk unknown to the young of other species. The possibility of becoming aware of their own overwhelming vulnerability in a disinterested, dangerous environment threatens too sudden and catastrophic an awakening.

During this period, even a false sense of safety is some measure of security. Retention of an innocent vision of living in a world in which all events have personal meaning provides the needed illusion of control. Believing that things happen because they are supposed to, or because someone makes them happen allows children the enchantingly reassuring vision of imagining that they have power and importance.

In such a world the child can still believe that his or her own wishes and actions affect the outcome of events that will later be understood to be in a category beyond personal influence. At least for a while, it's a needed comfort for the child to believe that the sun comes up each morning because "it's supposed to" or because "it's time for *me* to get up." So too the sun sets each evening because (like me) "it gets tired" or because "it's time for *me* to go to bed."

For most of recorded history, even adult understandings of the workings of nature have required a reassuringly pseudo-innocent perspective. Scientific understanding of the irrelevance of the human presence to what we call the sun's "rising and setting" comes late in our history.

This demythologizing is almost more than even an enlightened grown-up can bear. A person can be a long way past childhood and still be intimidated by an overwhelming sense of powerlessness and insignificance when faced with a head-on view of our place in the universe.

Let yourself take it in. You are a single creature among billions, a biological accident alive for a cosmic moment. Standing on a particular planet revolving mindlessly within the interplay of gravitational forces, we experience day and night, and the changing seasons only because of the effects of the spin of this mass on its axis and in its orbit around the sun relative to our limited vantage point.

This heliocentric view alone would be enough to overwhelm you. Expanding it to see even this "universe" as no more than a microcosm boggles the mind. How are we to tolerate the implications of our being only one of millions of such solar systems in a galaxy that is itself only one of millions of galaxies?

I liked it better when I still believed in the power of my wishes in a universe in which I had special importance. For just a little while I was certain that I could alter the weather just by chanting:

> Rain, rain, go away.
> Little Shelly wants to play.
> Rain, rain, go away.
> Come again some other day.

Clinging to pseudo-innocence is a way of denying realization of just how powerless we all are. As we outgrow the authentic innocence of childhood, we are confronted with the overwhelming realities of grown-up life. This disenchantment comes of learning, as we must,

. . . that we cannot influence many people; that we count for little; that the values to which our parents devoted their lives are to us insubstantial and worthless; that we feel ourselves to be . . . insignificant to other people and, therefore, not worth much to ourselves. . . .[1]

The self-protection of individual pseudo-innocence can serve as a temporary means of reassuring ourselves that we need not be helplessly vulnerable. By stubbornly ignoring the disappointment of our lives as they are, we can go on believing that Life is the fairy tale we want it to be. In such a storybook world, we can once more restore the hope that accompanies illusions of being someone special.

Once again we can believe that we have a significant place in an ultimately fair universe. Virtue will be rewarded and evil punished. We can *make* someone take care of us. To actualize that power, we need only be good.

But if we are to go on growing, increasing our freedom to find what happiness we might in the world as it is, each of us must go through repeated losses of innocence. The threshold of each new stage of life involves such a crisis. Additionally there are the almost daily small losses that seem a natural part of growing up. They continue throughout our adult lives as well. It behooves us to learn to make our way through this mixed bag of a life without allowing them any more attention than we have to. Perhaps wisdom is no more than surrender to what we cannot change without making things any worse by expecting more or less than what life provides.

All the important transitions seem too painful to endure without the protection of the temporary hedge of making believe that life is the fairy tale we might wish it to be. When the crises occur too early, or come upon us too savagely, or must be faced in an atmosphere of emotional hypocrisy, the needed protection of pretending may go on to become an enduring way of life.

The neurotic lifestyles that constitute being stuck in such pseudo-innocent postures involve a great deal of needless suffering. The burden of an exaggerated sense of self-importance and the handicap of a naïve understanding of what will bring happiness bring on avoidable disappointments and exaggerated suffering. The Pollyanna's ineffectual denial of real dangers makes it easy to get hurt needlessly. At the other end of the spectrum, the paranoid who mistakes being frightened for being in danger lives an overprotected, limited life of distorted vigilance. In either case, by paying so much attention to what others think and feel, we risk missing knowing what we really want for ourselves.

For those who choose saintliness as their pseudo-innocent posture, an exorbitant price is paid for appearing to be so good. Surface inauthenticity is counterbalanced by a proportionally grotesque caricature of hidden viciousness. Neither the "good souls" themselves nor those of us who are hurt by them are prepared for the outbreaks of unexpected destructiveness that punctuate the lives of those who are too good to be true.

All conscious attitudes are compensated by their opposites. The more extreme and seemingly "pure" the attitude, the more destructive its unconscious consequences. Clearly these neurotic instances of pseudo-innocence involve make-believe that has got far out of hand. The cost of pretending that one is not pretending eventually outweighs its benefits. But neurosis is not the only form of innocence for adults.

Periodic immersion in individual acknowledged fantasy is another form of innocence for all adults. If participation is conscious and if the daydreamer remains aware that this is a deliberate experience of momentary make-believe, such wishful indulgence need not be self-deluding.

Another relatively safe buffer against the pain of individual disenchantment is the protection afforded by participation in collective or communal innocence. A group member may temporarily abandon the boundaries between practical reality and wishful fantasy, as in the momentary surrender of critical judgment. Through acceptance of culturally sanctioned myths and fairy tales, this permits celebration of shared fantasies from which a person can later withdraw once more to the privacy of personal perspective.

Even the most primitive tribe has its well-developed oral tradition of enchanting stories. There are usually two kinds of stories, one held to be more central and significant than the other. In this book I have been concerned with the lesser stories, those folk-tale fictions told to entertain or to amuse. These naïve romances called fairy tales are sentimental accounts that often pivot on traditional conventions of

. . . mysterious birth, oracular prophecies about the future contortions of the plot, foster parents, adventures which involve capture by pirates [witches or worse], narrow escapes from death, recognition of the true identity of the hero and eventual marriage with the heroine.[2]

In addition to these fairy tales, each society has a more honored set of stories that illustrate the primary concerns of the culture. Early in the development of any particular society, these foundation tales are not recognized as myths or even as being of human origin. Rather, they constitute the basis of the group's religion and are thought of as revelations. The myths are sacred stories about the gods and demons themselves, and their preoccupation with human behavior. The settings sometimes include our origins out of heaven and hell, those worlds above and below this central place, the earth.

Whenever one culture supersedes another, the gods of the vanquished group become the demons of the conquerors. What was originally classical mythology becomes fable or folklore. As its metaphors lose their power, a group's mythology becomes relegated to the secular literature of fairy tale. In contemporary Western culture, Old Testament biblical mythology is gradually becoming demythologized in just that way.

Restoring the original power to these old tales of spiritual adventure has been the chosen task of that extraordinary contemporary mythologist, Joseph Campbell.[3] He has defined the myth as having four functions.[4] First there is the *mystical* or *metaphysical* attempt at a "reconciliation of consciousness with a precondition of its own existence . . . the monstrous nature of this terrible game that is life." [5] The second function is the *cosmological*, a mythic rendering of the universe that allows us to make sense of where we live. The *sociological* third function of myth is the validation and preservation of some specific social order.

It is Campbell's fourth, *psychological* function of mythology that is most relevant to fairy tales:

Here he sees a myth as a guide and support to bear individuals from birth to death through the difficult transitions which human life demands. This is perhaps the major function for Campbell, since he sees sociological and cosmological orders varying and those functions of mythology being contingent on the order of the time. Yet he feels there is an irreducible biology of the species which makes necessary that each man face the same inherent psychological problems. His emphasis is on the overly long period of immaturity and dependency of the human species and the consequent difficulties in crossing the threshold to adult responsibility, the difficulty in the delivery to a second birth, which is indeed a social birth. So it is that Campbell tells us "the fourth function is to initiate the individual into orders of his own psyche, guiding him toward his own spiritual enrichment and realization." [6]

Watered down or truncated as fairy tales may be, in the education of the young they continue to fulfill these residual mythical functions. Like acceptance of the mythological universe, belief in the fairy-tale world creates an illusion of form and harmony in an otherwise disorderly and imperfect life. And like myths, fairy tales support the expectation of that special sort of world order in which human beings have a central role.

So it is that fairy tales of childhood have a certain didactic authority that parallels the sacred instruction of the myths of adult religion. The Genesis story of the fall warns against the loss of innocence that comes with challenging the concept that someone else knows what is best for us. Individual yielding to temptation in the spirit of personal growth and adventure is always a challenge to the authority of the elders. In a society founded on religious beliefs, the seeking of secular wisdom is always viewed as sin. What the newly conscious individual experiences as freedom, the authorities define as disobedience.

Perhaps the priestly caste need not be so concerned. Even with the cosmic connection unplugged, the fairy tales continue to project the holy messages of the myths. In the long run, secular wisdom ends up being no more than a form of *communal innocence*.

Kept in perspective as just another form of pretending, communal innocence offers a collective shelter against individual disenchantment. However, uncritical acceptance of the feeling of belonging and the mutual dependence offered by such consensual validation involves risking the closed-minded constraints of mistaking the group's parochial outlook for *the one true vision* of what is normal, natural, or real. Communal innocence may blind a person to the *equivalence* of the multiple realities that can otherwise be experienced in a pluralistic society.

In the army, I found myself in a peculiar assemblage of differing "realities." For a while I was assigned to a military mental hygiene facility at Fort Carson, Colorado. Among the enlisted personnel that staffed the clinic all the psychologists and social workers came from "ethnic" backgrounds. I was the resident Jew. Additionally we had a Harlem black, a nisei who had grown up in the United States detention camps for Japanese-Americans, and a second oriental from San Francisco's Chinatown. We also boasted residents of Little Italy, Irish Shantytown, and other inbred ethnic enclaves.

One lunch hour we sat around comparing our contrasting childhood experiences and beliefs. Sitting with us, filled with silent wonder, was our token W.A.S.P. This commissioned psychiatrist came from a homogeneous midwestern town in which members of his own

Northern European Protestant denomination made up almost the entire population. Noting his silence, after a while I asked, "Hey, Captain, what's it like growing up in a Middle America White Anglo-Saxon Protestant family?" He thought the matter over with some care. Finally, out of the security of unquestioned communal innocence came his colorlessly self-assured reply: "Growing up in my family in our home town was . . . well, you know, just *regular*."

It had never occurred to him that alternatives to his personal experiences were valid equivalents of his own way of life! Trustingly unexamined collective attitudes such as his parallel their unlikely counterparts in the pseudo-innocent bigotry of "good old boys," the closed-mindedness of Marxist idealists, and the "bad vibe" avoidance of "heavy-headed" hippies.

No matter how shadowy their illusions, it is the only reality they know. Homogenized groups of communally innocent people share mutually supported perspectives about which they tolerate no challenge. Plato's Parable of the Cave [7] memorably depicts this collective solidarity.

Plato asks us to imagine people chained in a cave from childhood, in such a way that all they can see is the wall that they face. Some distance above and behind them a fire burns. Between the fire and the backs of the prisoners is a low wall. Just behind this wall other men pass in a steady stream. Above their heads they carry all sorts of figures made of wood and stone. The figures are held high enough to appear over the wall.

As a result, on the wall that they face, all that the prisoners can see of these objects is their shadows cast by fire. These shadows make up the imprisoned group's communally shared reality, their unquestioned world of sense experience. They all see it the same way. It's the only world they know.

Next, Plato invites us to imagine that one of these prisoners is unchained from this forced perspective of communal innocence. Once free to see the objects and firelight that cause these images to be cast, he will know that the other prisoners have mistaken shadows for reality.

Should he then return to enlighten his fellow prisoners, what would their reaction be? Knowing only their world of shadows, they would never believe him. His attempts to instruct them would be met with ridicule. If he seriously challenged their unquestioned beliefs, they might tear him to pieces.

The communally innocent group resists any sort of pluralism, readily sacrificing any deviant individual for the good of group solidarity. But punitive social sanctions are not the only risks faced by the misfit. It is difficult for the independent individual to maintain confidence in his or her personal beliefs when faced with going it alone. The compelling quality of deceptively innocuous communal agreement can be both intimidating and seductively corrupting.

As a kid, any time I expressed a feeling or a belief that differed from the family fairy-tale world, my mother would challenge me by demanding: "Tell me, *nisht-guteh* [no good one], can the whole world be crazy and only you sane?"

In the face of such a challenge it was difficult not to be overwhelmed with self-doubt. I endured a great deal of needless suffering by joining her in discrediting my own individual experiences in favor of the communal illusions. It took a long while before I realized that, Yes! there would be times when I was right even if no one else saw it my way. Years later I was delighted to run across George Bernard Shaw's wonderful line: "Fifty million Frenchmen can't be right!"

Once having learned to stand alone against a group, at first I expected to be able to face down those more innocent people. I was tempted to believe that they would have to recognize my advantage over them, admire me, and allow me special privileges. Ironically, usually the converse turns out to be true.

Having a freer vision than others allows us to be bolder than they might be. Consequently we make mistakes that they do not risk making. As a result they condemn us as fools, or worse. Their consolidated criticism may convince us to yield to their pressures, to close our eyes to new possibilities, and to live the safer, surer, more restricted life that their blindness demands.

In a symbolic short story titled "The Country of the Blind," [8] H. G. Wells warns us of the menace of communal innocence. Fifty years ago, Wells wrote of a mysterious mountain valley in South America that had been cut off from the rest of the world by a natural disaster. Settlers had come to this uninhabited valley in the long-ago past. A strange disease came upon them that from then on caused all of their children to be born blind.

Life was so very easy in the valley that gradually the blind children scarcely noticed their loss. The simple life in this abundant Eden made adaptation so easy that after fifteen generations this community of the blind had come to live without awareness of their handicap. Their forebears had arranged everything to fit their blindness:

Each of the radiating paths of the valley area had a constant angle to the others, and was distinguished by a special notch upon its kerbing; all obstacles and irregularities of path or meadow had long since been cleared away; all their methods and procedures arose naturally from their special needs.[9]

Their waking period was now the night which they called "day." During what we call the day, they slept. In seeming compensation for their blindness the remaining senses had become marvelously acute, allowing them to judge the slightest gesture of another person as far as seven paces away.

Intonation had long replaced expression with them, and touches, gesture, and their work with hoe and spade and fork was as free and confident as garden work can be.[10]

Until the day a stranger suddenly appeared, the people who lived in the country of the blind had not had any contact with outsiders since their arrival. While acting as a guide for an exploring party, a mountaineer from Bogotá was caught in a landslide. Nunez survived his fall into the valley and was discovered by the settlers.

Recognizing quickly that these people were blind, Nunez thought to find himself at great advantage. Instead he found that they soon came to consider *him* handicapped. They moved through the darkness with grace and confidence along paths on which he stumbled uncertainly and sometimes fell. With patronizing concern their leader asked:

"Must you be led like a child? Cannot you hear the path as you walk? Nunez laughed. "I can see it." . . .

"There is no such word as *see*," said the blind man, after a pause. "Cease this folly, and follow the sound of my feet." . . .

"Has no one told you, 'In the country of the Blind the One-eyed Man is King?' "

"What is blind?" asked the blind man carelessly over his shoulder.[11]

After much argument, Nunez gave up trying to get them to acknowledge his superiority. Isolated by his understanding of things they did not acknowledge, lonely and insecure, at times doubting his own sanity, eventually he narrowed his concerns to one central longing. He wanted only to become one of them. He begged them to forgive his fumbling ways and accept his as a citizen of the country of the blind.

Nunez had fallen in love with one of the young women of the valley and wished to spend his life there. Her family and others in the community opposed the marriage because they thought of him as a peculiarly incompetent and inadequate human being.

It was an uneasy time in the valley. Among the tribal elders of the valley lived a medicine man, greatly respected for his deep thinking. When his counsel was sought, he came up with an idea for curing Nunez's peculiarities. After meditating on the problem, out of his patriarchal wisdom the medicine man counseled:

Those queer things that are called the eyes, and which exist to make an agreeable soft depression in the face, are diseased, in the case of . . . [Nunez], in such a way as to affect his brain. They are greatly distended, and his eyelids move, and consequently his brain is in a state of constant irritation and destruction. . . . And I think I may say with reasonable certainty that, in order to cure him completely, all that we need do is a simple and easy surgical operation—namely to remove these irritant bodies.[12]

At first Nunez was horrified by the idea of having his eyes cut out. But soon he began to doubt himself. How could he be sure that he knew better than they just what was real and what wasn't? After all, he was the only one in the valley who stumbled about. All the others moved with sureness and grace. When he turned to the woman he loved for confirmation, she could only cry joyfully at the thought that her lover might yet be made whole and normal, that together they might live like everyone else.

It was so painful to be a misfit, an outsider. Nunez wanted to marry this woman, but almost more than that he wanted to be accepted as one of the community. It was so hard to go on trusting himself when no one else saw things his way. Could they really all be crazy and only he sane?

It was so difficult to keep clear in his mind that the only reason that he made more mistakes than they did was because he was aware of more possibilities. As a sighted person in this valley of the blind, he had thought he would be king. Instead, his ability to see things as they were resulted in those who could not see making him into the fool. It took all of his strength for Nunez to turn away from their offer to restore his health. The lonely dangerous climb out of that happy valley was his only way of escaping the temptation of their offer of acceptance.

Group pressure to give up individual variation from communal innocence continues to be girded by punitive sanctions from the authorities. We may wish to believe that the punishment of heresy ended with long-ago barbarisms like the Spanish Inquisition. But official instances still exist, ranging from the brutal Soviet psychiatric incarceration of political dissidents to our own maintenance of those outdated nuisance ordinances called Blue Laws.

The tyranny of the group is proportional to its members' pseudo-innocent belief that they know what's best for the individual. Thinking of themselves as the good guys, the group cannot understand why anyone would resist their offer to look after the poor lost soul. The encounter groups spawned by the Human Potential movement during the sixties and early seventies make clear that the coercive pressures of communal innocence are as alive and well intentioned as ever. Here is one man's account of his own escape from being saved:

Several years ago I participated in a sensitivity group which met twice a week for about six weeks. It was the fourth meeting, and I was being briefed on what had transpired during the previous session, which I had missed. The intense young man who was doing the briefing was somewhat annoyed at me for having been absent on that occasion and told me so (our group had two prime rules: regular attendance and complete honesty). Then he came to the heart of the matter:

"Last week we all told what was most important in our lives. Do you have something that is most important to you?"

"Yes," I replied.

"What is it?"

"It's none of your business."

It wasn't my intention to be so blunt, but since honesty was the order of the day I rose to the occasion and told him what I felt. He was truly shocked, as though I had violated some ancient code—as though I didn't have the right to withhold information from the group. I can't remember what was said after that; all I recall is the look of complete incomprehension that covered his face.[13]

Without recognizing our own gullibility, we may be caught up in aspects of communal innocence that seriously curtail our own individual freedoms and discredit the integrity of our personal identities. Like racism, sexism is a powerful contemporary example of oppressive communal innocence. In both instances, unwittingly the victims become vulnerable to blaming themselves for brutality that has been perpetrated upon them.

As a feminist therapist, part of my job is validating the heresy of these victims. My work with Ellen is a clear instance of this irony. Very much a creature of our time, she began psychotherapy in the midst of a struggle to transform her life from total immersion in the caretaking role of housewife/mother to that of a full-grown woman, a second-career-oriented, late-coming graduate student seeking a life of her own. Like many other such women she had long been devoted and long been depressed. Now engaged in an increasingly determined rekindling of her brightness, imagination, and personal initiative, she often feels guilty, intimidated, and greatly overwhelmed.

She entered her therapy session late that morning, out of breath, looking harassed, but obviously pleased to have reached what she calls her "resting-place" once more. "It's been one of those days," she began. In addition to the usual whirl of competing intentions, activities, and demands, this weekend she and her husband had bought, equipped, and stocked an aquarium tank for one of the children. Of course, some of the equipment did not work, there was no practical place to keep the tank as yet, the scavenging catfish had eaten some of the baby fish, and one of the more expensive specimens had flung itself out of the tank and onto the floor during the night. This last bit of unexpected suicide necessitated not only getting rid of the body, but also announcing the death to, and dealing with the grief of, the mourning child.

All of this led Ellen into a seemingly escapist fantasy about what it would be like to live in an aquarium herself, free from responsibility and taken care of by someone else. But as she began to describe what she hoped would be a free and pleasant existence, the fantasy began being reshaped by some of the stresses and contingencies of her own less-than-pleasant life. At first, she saw herself looking up from the bottom of the tank at the beautiful and expensive specimens of fish swimming freely near the surface, the sunlight filtering through their colorful tails. They reminded her of her husband and myself, both of whom she very much "admires."

But it turned out that she herself remained hidden down in the shadows in a corner of the tank. She saw herself as the scavenging catfish, an ugly creature whom the petshop salesman had urged them to buy because it would clean up the tank garbage.

Though Ellen began by admiring us, she quickly came to wanting to bite off our heads. The more she looked at these flamboyant male fish, the more they began to look like "cocks" to her. And soon enough wanting to bite their heads off became wanting to bite our cocks off.

This association was obviously upsetting to Ellen, and so she trailed off into safer areas, recounting how all this reminded her of the time long ago when she was a little girl seeing her brothers walking around with erections, and somehow connecting the fascinating flamboyance of their phallic pride with her overall envy of their general freedom. The session ended without further elaboration.

During the next session, after some initial seeming digressions into how difficult it was to be housewife/mother/graduate student all at the same time, she returned more directly to the fantasy. Ellen acknowledged that she was uneasy about how peculiar the fantasy was becoming and about what my reactions might be, and so she had tried to put her mind elsewhere, only to be drawn back to that inner space again and again.

She went on with the fantasy. The image of biting off the cocks, elaborated by some historical associations, had transformed the fantasy into that of being the recipient of the first penis organ-transplant in history. This was an exciting prospect but one which she felt would pose many problems. She would have to wear full skirts to hide her secret. Otherwise people would ask questions about this transplanted penis, questions to which she would have no answer because she would not even understand the questions.

Another upsetting aspect to the acquisition of this new and unfamiliar organ was that she was sure she would be terribly lonely. Not only would her secret separate her from others, but she would have to do without lovemaking. She did fantasize that someday if the penis became long enough she might be able to screw herself. But for now there was no way to enjoy this promising appendage because the transplant area was still too sore from the sutures.

Ellen expressed a good deal of anxiety at having this fantasy. She was afraid that I would find her too crazy. And, being sophisticated enough to be familiar with the Freudian vision of women as castrated, penis-envying inferiors, she was afraid that the fantasy might reduce her life-and-death struggle in my eyes to the neurotic demandingness of some nutty dame who just wanted to be a man.

But my interpretation was *not* that she wanted to become a man, and consequently suffered from *penis envy,* but that she simply wanted a life of her own and what she was expressing was *person envy.* I told her it seemed to me that the anxiety expressed along with her fantasy was unwarranted, because her longings constituted no danger to men. The metaphor of the penis transplant reflected no fundamental Freudian (or other) biological/psychic rip-off transformation. It was but a culturally determined, misleadingly symbolic expression of her legitimate human longings to fulfill her own purposes. And what's more, I told her clearly that I was sure that the loneliness inherent in her courageous transformation would be overcome once the soreness of transition gave way to a comfortable recognition of all that she could be.[14]

Ellen is one of the many casualties of the politically oppressive aspect of communal innocence. So long as she believes in the patriarchal myths and the sexist fairy tales inherent in the reassuring seeming-certainty of our conventional wisdom, she must pay the price of discrediting her own immediate experience and judgment. The feminist position offers Ellen a way of interpreting her feelings and her fantasies other than the depersonalizing outlook of the dominant authority.

Sometimes it is difficult for any of us to see that there are more personal options, and that it is all right for us to choose them in place of what communal standards have taught us is "the right way." We may not be able to see that we have an alternative until it is offered by someone else whom we have invested with great power. In order to become self-validating we must learn this basic truth over and over again until we need not depend on anyone else to have to remind us that we may do as we please. Sometimes it's hard to know whether we have escaped *out of* or *into* the country of the blind. Many years ago the title drew me to a book called *The God That Failed*[15] in which several intellectuals had written of their disenchantment with Communism. What intrigued me most was that, either before or after their Marxist disaffection, many of them suffered a similarly flawed romance with Catholicism.

It is possible to be sane and yet to imagine that you are crazy. But it's also possible to be crazy without knowing it. There are times when you believe that you are the only one who is sane, and even those may turn out to be times when you were really crazy.

Getting out from between the polarities would help. Some dilemmas seem unresolvable: What is real and what unreal? Who is sane and who insane? When am I doing the right thing and when the wrong?

Who knows? My only hope lies in allowing myself to lose interest in finding the answer. At those times when I find myself at peace I realize that it's only because "I forgot the question."

Even having abandoned trying to answer the Big Questions, I still insist on trying to judge the more immediate everyday issues.

The origins of the conflicts which I experience between myself and others is to be found in the fact that too often *I do not know what I feel, I do not say what I mean,* and *I do not do what I say.* It is in large part a matter of being honest with myself.[16]

When I am able to straighten out where I stand with myself, I still may not know just where I stand with others. Most of us choose to spend our time with people whose expressed beliefs are congruent with our own. During the senseless suffering of Vietnam, I couldn't understand why it took so long for the pressure of public opinion to result in the withdrawal of American troops. Everyone *I* knew was *against* the war! It was almost impossible for me to comprehend that for so long the vast majority of the people in this country really believed in a reality so different from the one I knew.

The reciprocal of this illusion occurs when individuals become disenchanted with traditionally held conventional wisdom without knowing how many others have also become irreverent. I am reminded of the results of a project conducted by a friend's social research company. A contract was let by the government for his firm to study the use of marijuana on a particular marine base.

The two findings that fascinated me most were: (1) the *majority* of marines questioned admitted that they smoked grass; (2) most members of that majority believed that they constituted a *minority!*

As children we all start out being taught by unconsciously self-serving adults that life is orderly and comprehensible. After a while experience instructs us that we simply did not understand what it was all about. As children grow, the community teaches them an agreed-upon system of conventional wisdom. Too soon some of us find out that this communal innocence serves us no better than our own original infantile innocence.

As adolescents, while insisting on asserting our individuality, we strike the defiant postures sanctioned by the teen-age subculture of our peers. Sooner than we expect, most of us "grow up and settle down." Once immersed in the style of adult conventional wisdom peculiar to our own particular generation, we imagine that we have progressed beyond our parents' naïve assumptions. A few of us hold out, transparently remaining misfits, without understanding that in the end we are all misfits.

Believing that the world is orderly and comprehensible is hazardous. Again and again, things turn out to be different from what they seemed. But maintaining recognition of our own insignificance in an ultimately unmanageable life is too overwhelming to bear for very long. Sharing group beliefs is restrictive. Individual perspectives are equally unreliable. We can never know for sure whether or not other people see things the way we do.

What proportion of the declared majority are privately disenchanted with beliefs they publicly affirm? How many of us who defiantly stand alone do so only because we do not know how to join the group? To what extent is outspoken disenchantment simply our particular way of finding a place in the community structure?

To what extent does our deviance serve the community? Who speaks for the voiceless? Who gets saddled with claiming as his or her own the skepticism that other group members pretend is foreign to them? Is the office of "town drunk" a voluntary or an appointed position? When "the village idiot" dies don't we always groom someone else to take his place?

If life has no inherent meaning, what would it be like to face our helplessness head-on in this unmanageable universe? One deceptively safe way to find out is to try rereading Lewis Carroll's *Alice's Adventures in Wonderland*.[17]

For more than a century this topsy-turvy tale of Alice's "journey to the end of the night"[18] has remained a captivating exploration of the underside of life for both children and adults. But it is curious to note that, typically, kids and grown-ups respond to this experience with consistently different reactions.

Though the story fascinates children, it usually frightens them, too. Like Alice herself, most kids refuse to accept the chaos of Wonderland for what it is. Innocently they cling to their assumption that all experience must be meaningful. But in Wonderland, insisting that "Everything's got a moral if only you can find it" simply deepens the visitor's sense of bewilderment and powerlessness.

Grown-ups almost inevitably find that, like life, Wonderland reduces them to laughing at the comic absurdity of their nonsensical situation. As life keeps coming at us, there are times when either we must laugh at ourselves or we will surely die of despair.

Throughout her adventuresome explorations of the maddeningly inconsistent world beneath everyday consciousness, Alice encounters one reversal after another. Strand by strand the entire fabric of her everyday approach to life seems to be coming apart. The failure of Alice's literal attempts to learn the rules for the order of things in lawless Wonderland vicariously guides the reader along the inevitably futile parallel metaphoric search for meaning in his or her own life.

It is simple curiosity that first makes Alice follow the White Rabbit down into the rabbit-hole. In no time at all the fearlessness of the innocent child has plunged her into a frightening situation in which usual modes of thought have no meaning at all. Familiar conventions of social exchange and language are no longer valid. Finally even those completely taken-for-granted fundamental dimensions of orderly time and predictable space are nowhere to be found in this nonsensical world of wonder.

Desperately chanting empty recitations of rote-learned lessons, Alice tries to translate the chaotic present into the familiar stability of the past. Falling helplessly down the rabbit-hole, she litanizes multiplication tables, tries to curtsy, and wonders what latitude she has arrived at (without knowing just exactly what is meant by a "latitude"). When Alice and some of the Wonderland animals emerge soaking from a pool of tears, they consider drying themselves by reciting a passage from a history textbook ("the driest thing I know").

Wonderland is a place where the everyday assumptions on which we usually depend turn out to be empty illusions that do not warrant our innocent attachment to them. Here animals talk. Inanimate things have personalities. Objects and symbols are interchangeable. Cause and effect no longer operate in only one direction. All our old familiar ideas prove ridiculously invalid and logic often leads us to incorrect conclusions.

Once Alice can no longer count on her beliefs making sense, she finds that along with her loss of security, she loses her identity. The same painfully perplexing question echoes throughout her adventures: "But then . . . who am I?"

As you will remember, Alice's difficulties culminate in a final test of Wonderland's rules, an irreverent courtroom scene in which "the Law" itself is on trial! For Alice underground and above-ground courts turn out to be too much alike. In both settings, order is arbitrary and inconsistent. Both systems of justice are incoherent and unfair. This similarity threatens Alice with the near realization that her own everyday world is just as chaotic a combination of anarchy and artifice as this terrifying subterranean nightmare.

Faced with an overwhelming loss of innocence, Alice turns toward the only salvation available to a child prematurely pushed to cross this awful threshold:

. . . complete and active denial of the horrible, unacceptable truth [19] . . . [as] a symbolic rejection of mad sanity in favor of the sane madness of ordinary existence.[20] . . .

Alice's quest for reasonable experience whisks her back to her only possible, albeit artificial, world where the ultimately irrational makes life sane. Thus, the book is paradoxically both a denial and an affirmation of order—a kind of catharsis of what can never be truly purged but what must, for sanity's sake, be periodically purged in jest, fantasy, or dream. The Wonderland creatures and their world are not a pack of cards, after all. They are, so to speak, more "real" than so-called reality. But waking life, as most of us know it, must function as if they are unreal, as if chaos is amusing "nonsense." [21]

As each of us faces the unmanageable life revealed by our disenchantment, like Alice we may be tempted to flee back to the reassuring "realities" offered by communal innocence. But whatever uneasiness we may experience in Wonderland, living a life that is not constrained by conventional wisdom means being on our own, with greater freedom to do as we please. That freedom is difficult to retain. It requires that we trust ourselves even when everyone else seems to agree that we don't know what we're doing.

11

Making the Best of It

Piece by piece, my original innocence has been surrendered. By now most of it is lost, strayed, or stolen. With eyes widening to see the world as it is, I have been forced to recognize that my personal existence lacks significance in this absurdly arbitrary, disarmingly unpredictable life. Now that I realize how little I matter, how am I to renew the hope and the courage I need if I am to go on?

It helps a little to remember that everyone else is in the same position as I find myself. Feeling alone, helpless, and afraid is merely the ordinary state of affairs. Remembering this helps, but not a whole lot.

No matter what the species, no creature is in a position to control its own life. Of all life forms, only human beings additionally are able to be aware of their predicament. We are free to know that too soon we will die, and that after a short while no one will even remember our having lived.

Other mammals appear able simply to enjoy being momentarily well fed, warm, and dry. At such times, only Homo sapiens are capable of worrying about whether or not the moment will last, of wondering what it is *really* all about, or of becoming distracted by comparing that moment with some other moment.

Consciousness makes it possible for us to imagine that things can be different from what they are. As a result we have made changes in our physical and social conditions, but in the long run neither art nor science has given lasting meaning to our lives. At this point we begin to recognize that some "advances" cause us to lose far more than we have gained.

Clearly, imagination is both the crown we wear and the cross we bear. Seeing how things might be allows us to begin to improve our lot. In the process, we give up simply accepting any good moment with grace. Instead, we become attached to intensifying the feeling, to prolonging the experience, and to multiplying its occurrence.

In retrospect we can see that whole cultures and philosophies have arisen, flourished, deteriorated, and disappeared. Still, imagination encourages our insistent clinging to the certainty that we can yet be happy ever after. For this we pay the price of the needless suffering that accompanies such pseudo-innocent pretending.

Living in the absence of illusion often seems unbearable. At such times it is hard not to give way to imagining our lives to be more what we would like them to be. Opening statements about such willful fantasies usually begin: "Well, personally I'd like to think that . . . ," *or* "It's just not fair. I don't see why it should have to be that way," *or* "I don't care what anybody says, I just can't accept that. . . ."

In trying to make our worlds more manageable, we each sometimes pretend to be more important than we really are. During periods of desperation even negative power will do. It is then that, unable to get our own way, we may settle for preventing other people from getting theirs.

We will do almost anything to create the illusion that our individual will counts for something. We dramatize our situations, see our particular roles as being special, strike heroic postures, and aspire to "higher things." But repeatedly our pseudo-innocent fantasies are interrupted by unwanted reminders that our stay is short, our position vulnerable, and our impact inconsequential.

Again and again we find ourselves aware once more that we are caught in what Ernest Becker calls "the total bind of life," [1] trapped in an unresolvable paradox. We cannot long escape the shocking self-consciousness that we are at the same time both the dreamers and the defecators, the lovers and the aggressors, the living and the dying.

It is this fall into self-consciousness that was the original sin of Adam and Eve. For a time, knowing that each had his or her own special place in Paradise, they had lived in comfortable innocence. Obediently unconscious, they would be taken care of by Someone who knew what was best for them. But once they ate from the Tree of Knowledge of Good and Evil, they became aware of both their vulnerabilities and their responsibilities. Once conscious, they were exiled to a place East of Eden, a world in which they would suffer the hardships of being on their own. It is that order of loss of innocence that lets people see that "the world as it really is, is devastating and terrifying. . . . it *makes routine, automatic, secure, self-confident-activity impossible. . . .*" [2]

Only then do we awaken to those existential anxieties that are inescapably part of everyone's life. Paul Tillich has described them as the dread that goes with awakening to how fate and death belie our fantasy that we control our lives, how the meaninglessness of life mocks our insistence that we are somehow special, and how our limited freedom and imperfect choices discredit our assertion that we are the good guys.[3]

In the years following World War II it became popular to be philosophically preoccupied with existential despair. Jean-Paul Sartre called our attention to the meaninglessness of a life into which we do not ask to be born, in which we are given a name, a family, and a history that we do not choose.

Several young French students believed they understood the implications of Sartre's disenchantment. Life had no meaning. All was despair. And so they chose death.

Unfortunately they had misunderstood Sartre. Irrevocably they had acted on that misunderstanding. Believing that the absence of inherent meaning in their lives left them no other option, these misguided Sartreans committed suicide. In contrast, Sartre himself understood that recognizing that there is no inherent meaning in life frees us to choose. We bring our own arbitrary meaning to our lives. "I choose man," Sartre announced and thereafter gave meaning to his own existence by living out the rest of his years as a Marxist.

Aware that life had no inherent meaning, Sartre was able to make the best of it by willingly surrendering to deliberate, conscious pretending. Without fooling himself into believing that he knew some higher truth, or that he had some bottom line on reality, Sartre allowed his sense of make-believe to transform the everyday events of his life into festivals.

Sartre found himself in the usual position of the haunted prophet. His task was to tell people the news that everyone secretly already

knew but that no one wanted to hear spoken aloud. Finding meaning in life, he declared, was no more than seeing new clothes on the
emperor. It was okay to dress him anyway you chose so long as you
understood that the only thing that clothed his nakedness was your
choosing one vision over another.

People had always known that they were cheating a bit in pretending greater belief than they actually experienced. Cheating is no
big deal, but it's one thing to bend the rules and quite another to
point out that all rules are arbitrary and unreal.

It is curious to note how much more lenient society is to the cheat than
to the spoil-sport. This is because the spoil-sport shatters the play-world
itself.[4]

People everywhere have always depended on the play of their
imagination to create order, form, and harmony in an otherwise
frustratingly ambiguous, often distressingly disinterested world.
Willing, and wisely, we sometimes *choose* to fool ourselves. In
every culture there are sanctioned ways of suspending critical judgment for the purpose of creative make-believe. Most offer lovely
rewards at minimal risk. Making-believe allows the fun of play, the
richness of poetic expression, the beauty of art, the power of sacra-
ment, and the joyful magic of celebration.

Into an imperfect world and into the confusion of life ·. . . [play] brings
a temporary limited perfection . . . [of] the arena, the card-table, the
magic circle, the temple, the stage . . . , the tennis court, [and] the court
of justice.[5]

Recognized as temporary ways of self-abandon to make-believe, all
these forms of creative play provide the sorts of illusion that make
tolerable a life that is otherwise discontinuous, unpredictable, and
senseless. But during such interludes, there is always the danger of
helplessly falling under the spell that was at first cast voluntarily
and once could be revoked at will. When one person seems to have
forgotten that this is make-believe, the other will urgently remon-
strate or reassure, "Hey, it's only a game," "We were just pretending," or "It's all right. It's all over now."

Losing our original innocence does not mean that we may never
again enjoy experiencing things the way we would have liked them

to be. Make-believe is wonderful. It is only the pseudo-innocence of pretending that we are not pretending that threatens us with needless suffering.

Consider, for example, a universal adult experience. From time to time all of us grown-ups feel weary of having to take care of ourselves. Especially during times of stress and unhappiness, what we need from one another is the opportunity to have the make-believe experience that we could be cared for as though we were still children.

At the end of a long, particularly difficult day, how good it is to be able to return to a mate, a lover, or a friend, to someone to whom it matters how we feel. Like a child we can come for parenting, and like a mother or father, the other can take us in. It's the sort of momentary comfort that may get both partners through a life that just keeps coming at us. Still we must not get so lost in the pretending that we forget that we are both really grown-ups and that neither knows what's best for the other.

Keeping this in focus requires that the one who is playing the parent that night not try to fix the other's broken world. The pretend parenting partner must not presume to take over or to tell the one who is playing at being the child what to do about the day's hurts. Rather than actually trying to take care of the other, that night's parent need only be personally available by being willing to listen with sympathetic understanding to the *feelings* expressed in the others' complaints. What needs to be communicated is:

I'm here and I care. I'm sorry you're having such a tough time. I'm willing to listen, to hurt because you hurt, and to be respectfully careful not to tell you how you should feel or what you should do.

If this can be done without forgetting that they are two grown-ups just making believe that one is smaller and more helpless than the other, then tonight's pretend parent can be tomorrow night's pretend child.

Like good theater, creative make-believe demands the temporary suspension of hard-headed, matter-of-fact practicality. Instead of coming as critics, we must be willing to pretend that we are a part of the play we are watching and, at least until the final curtain, that the happenings on the stage are that evening's reality.

Like all metaphors, the theater is a flawed image for this param-
eter of everyday life. The audience's boundary is distinct. Watching
the evening's performance is a clearly separate experience from life
outside the theater. The border between personal fantasy and our
actual lives is less clear. It is impossible to know for sure when I am
seeing the world as it is, and when I am seeing it as I believe it should
be. Even now, I cannot be certain that my cautionary tales in the
second part of this book are any more than latter-day fairy tales.

If you have been willing to pretend to believe them innocently,
you may have experienced something of value for yourself. Yet you
know that it would have been dangerous for you to have believed so
completely that you imagined that I know best. Someone once suggested that in listening to a fairy tale

. . . the child should not "believe" the story he is told; he should not
disbelieve it either, but send out imaginative roots into that mysterious
world between the "is" and the "is not" which is where his own ultimate
freedom lies.[6]

For a long, long time I tried to figure out what I could believe in
and what I could not. Fortunately, I eventually gave up in despair.
I find that the only way to solve some problems is by losing serious
interest in them. Whenever I become obsessively immersed in resolving metaphysical issues, I end up feeling bad. Self-doubt and depression always rush in to fill the voids created by the unattainable answers such questions seem to demand. Even if I could settle such
matters, how would it help me to know for sure that something was
Real or Unreal, Good or Bad, True or False, any more than it could
help to know whether I am Selfish or Unselfish, Fair or Unfair, Deserving or Undeserving of happiness. So long as I pay attention to
such questions, I will remain in the sort of trouble that chronically
burdens only the innocent.

When I desperately pursue final answers to ultimate questions, I
end up depressed. On the other hand, when I strike the pseudo-
innocent pose of the consummate cynic, the jaded apathy that ensues
is no more pleasant than my depression.

Fortunately, there is another alternative. Knowing that there is
nothing special about my own quite ordinary helplessness and insignificance, and understanding that life is too important a matter to be
taken fully seriously, I am free to *play at* being innocent. Happily I

surrender to creative flights of imagination without losing sight of the fact that I am simply pretending. Knowing that there is no inherent meaning in my life, nor any right way for me to live, I am free to act *as if* what I do or say really matters.

There is little danger in my deliberate indulgence in playing at being innocent from time to time, so long as I remain clear that *I don't believe in anything.* Paradoxically it is just this shameless disregard for any particular "reality" that leaves me free to say as well that *I believe in everything.* Once I understand that nothing matters and that all paths are equivalent, I need only choose one or another that works for me during that particular time of my life.

Science, religion, politics, and philosophy are all simply metaphoric ways of looking at the aimless ongoing stream of life. Each of these perspectives is no more than a reassuring hedge that lets us imagine that we might dam, direct, or at the very least be able to chart the chaotic course of its current. No matter how elaborate, none serves as any more than a tale told to ease our journey.

Knowing that no way of looking at life is any more real than another, at any given moment I am willing to commit my faith to any set of metaphors that makes my life more exciting, my experiences more colorful, my relationships richer. Never do I willingly attribute any more significance than that to all the wonderfully hokey imagery to which I bring my energy and my devotion.

In this air of playfulness I have given myself to philosophy, to religion, and to magic. Marxism and Existentialism, Hasidism and Zen, Tarot and the I Ching have each been lovely, wondrous spiritual adventures. Each engaged me for a while. Each left me transformed. Whether or not God exists, believing in Him (or Her) has been an awesome journey. No metaphor is more powerful. As my life goes on, I hope to believe again as deeply in other fairy tales, to believe in each new one for however long they enrich my experience.

The paths I choose are partly determined by vulnerability to what trends are sanctioned by the counter-culture with which I most comfortably identify. Had I lived in America a century earlier, I doubt that I would have become fascinated with Far Eastern ideology.

Temperament also plays its part. As an intuitive type, I am drawn most easily to the nonrational and to the mysterious. As an introvert, I find the communal innocence of myth and institutionalized religion less compelling than the individual romance of my own personal dreams and the solitary wanderings in the uncharted territory of my own inner space.

For most of my adult life I have been immersed in the soul-searching pilgrimage of psychotherapy, first as a patient, then as a therapist (and at times as a patient once more). This long psychic/spiritual journey has helped me to understand that the personal struggle to make the best of an unmanageable life may follow any path that suits a particular traveler at any particular time along his or her way.

Everything works. Nothing works for very long. Unwittingly I stumble onto a particular path. Once I recognize what I have blundered onto, next it is necessary for me consciously and deliberately to choose to do what I am already doing. I follow that path until it seems to go nowhere, then wander in despair for a time only to discover that I have blundered onto yet another path.

Again it is time to accept responsibility without blame for this next phase of the journey that Chance has charted. Often I don't deliberately *make* the significant decision. Instead I come to realize that somewhere along the way the decision has already been made. At that point, I need only surrender, responsibly accepting the choice as my own, or risk spending the rest of my days fleeing from my life as it is.

In every important aspect of my life, I have found myself delivered into situations I did not choose, discovered attitudes in myself of which I was unaware, and been forced to abide by decisions I only later discovered that I myself had made. Sometimes, I refuse to accept my plight. Other times, I surrender with grace. Each time I find that I must struggle again with my willful attachment to innocence.

The most recent segment of this journey has involved my having to deal with the threat of an early death. It is only one example of the lifelong twisting and turning needed to hedge against helplessness in the face of the full impact of my losses of innocence. I must learn to accept these if I am to avoid still more needless suffering, and if I am to receive what is offered of the joys of personal growth and freedom.

Like most people, during the first half of my life I had given

little serious thought to the fact that someday I would die. I entered
my thirties innocent of such morbid concerns. Within less than four
years of my own thirtieth year to heaven, my wife and I lost all of
our parents. One year her mother died, the next year my father, then
her father, and months later my mother.

All during that emotionally catastrophic period and for a long
while afterward, bewilderment and grief were the leitmotifs of our
lives. Before those hammer blows fell, I had long thought of myself
as a powerful, competent, live-forever husband-father-psychothera-
pist. Suddenly I felt like a painfully vulnerable overgrown orphan.
At times it seemed as though everyone around me was dying. Any
minute, I might be next.

Each of my parents' funerals seemed a grotesque amalgam of
sanctimony, sentimentality, and low comedy. These traditional cere-
monies were conducted by rabbis who had never met my folks, and
catered by "funeral chapels" that exploited the vulnerability of the
mourners.

These experiences turned my attention to the inevitability of my
own death. Though not yet faced with my own eventual life-
threatening illness, still in the flush of good health, I decided to make
plans for the event that would eliminate all the distasteful cere-
monial and commercial aspects of death. There would be no funeral,
no burial, and no gravesite. I decided to donate my body to science.
Foregoing any organ-bank heroics, I'd simply arrange to have my
body handed over to a medical school to be used as an anatomy-class
cadaver.

It took me several weeks to find out what arrangements I needed
to make. Finally, one morning my mail included the necessary forms
from the National Society for Medical Research. Now all I needed
to do was to sign a statement certifying that with full knowledge of
my next of kin, I willingly donated my body (after death) to a particular local school of medicine.

For almost two years these papers lay unsigned in a pigeonhole
of my cluttered rolltop desk. Mostly I ignored them. Occasionally I
made excuses to myself (and to others when they would listen), just
why it was taking me so long to complete this simple straightforward
transaction.

Trying to be sensible and realistic about the whole thing, again and again I announced bravely that it was because I was afraid to die. But admitting that I was avoiding facing up to this dread of my own inevitable death just didn't help.

For a long while nothing helped. Slowly I began to sense a peculiar sort of vulnerability and with it growing awareness of my underlying unconscious fantasy of immortality. I began to realize that my real reason for putting off signing these forms was the avoidance of future embarrassment!

All at once I could see the whole terrible tableau. The scene took place in a medical school anatomy lab only hours after my death. My body lay inert under a sterile white sheet. The professor began his lecture. All the while the students tried to look as though they were listening attentively. But having been through this many times before, the professor was aware of the students' repeated nervous glances toward the covered cadaver. At last it was time. The professor pulled back the sheet. Suddenly *I* felt awful. I looked so fat. I could have died of embarrassment. The day after I became aware of that fantasy, I signed the forms and mailed them in.

I thought that the matter had been settled once and for all. I had arranged an opportunity for friends and family to mourn my passing by suggesting that when I died they should get together to hold a workshop, a sort of memorial encounter group. It was not until years later that I reconsidered that last bit of pseudo-innocent postmortem management of mine. A friend of mine instructed me. In a state of uneasy enthrallment I had listened to this recently widowed woman's disturbingly moving account of how she and her grown children had washed and dressed her husband's body in preparation for his burial. Before he died, this was not the sort of tender farewell in which any of them would have imagined being a part. Now it was an experience that would mean a great deal to all of them for the rest of their lives.

I found listening to her account terribly unsettling. I respected this woman and the value of what she had undertaken. Still I could not imagine having my family do that with my body when I died, nor could I conceive of my wishing to wash and dress the body of anyone I loved. Unable to discredit what this woman had been through, and reluctant to reconsider my long unchallenged decision about the disposal of my own body, I struggled for many hours against my need to reopen the whole matter.

As I began to face the issues once more, I realized that any insistence that I be in control of my body after I die is no more than continued pseudo-innocent clinging to my fantasy of immortality. Facing yet another bit of my ultimate helplessness, I acknowledged that what happens to my body after I die is none of my business! I let my family know that all bets were off. It will be up to the living to decide what is best for them to do with my body.

After our parents died, both my wife and I broke with our extended families. After a while it seemed that there was no one important left in our lives who was old enough to die. My preoccupation with my own mortality faded into the background until, at forty, I became seriously ill.[7]

I have written in detail elsewhere [8] of the earliest phases of my struggles against the loss of my innocent belief that I could live for as long as I chose. Like everyone else, cognitively I understood that someday I would die and that there was nothing of significance that I could do about it. But until I was faced with the imminence of my dying, I did not realize how desperately I still clung to the belief that *somehow* I would not die until I was ready.

My first neurosurgical ordeal would have been enough to compel me to reexamine the whole matter of my helplessness in the face of a foreshortened life. The second bout of neurosurgery followed three years after the first, the heart attack three years after that. During those years I was doing my best to learn to accept my life as it was. Knowing that my time seemed increasingly limited, I had decided to try to make the best of it.

Now that I recognized that I had a choice, I reexamined my relationships and my activities. I had to decide whether or not these were the people with whom I wanted to spend what time I had, and if these were the ways I wanted to invest my limited energies. It felt good to realize how much of my life was already what I wanted it to be. My family and my friends turned out to be the ones I would have wanted. My work as a psychotherapist, the patients I chose, and my writing all suited me well. I already was who I wanted to be.

During that time of restoring vitality to my life temporarily I had to define myself as a sick man who hadn't long to live. Objectively it wasn't hard to do. This definition was readily confirmed by my doctors and by all the life insurance companies who had turned me down. Subjectively it meant that other people might shun me as a pariah, write me off as done for, or patronize me out of pity. Taking on the stigmatized identity of an ill or dying person also left me limited by the crochety irritability that comes with feeling brittle and fragile. Still, after a time I often could honestly answer the question "How are you?" with the paradoxical reply "Fine, except for my health."

I had it down. I'd learned well how to be he who walked in the shadow of death and yet could say, "I am *not* dying, I am living."

During these seven years since my first operation, I have written eight books. Each time I do the next piece of work on my self I discover some new aspect of my struggle against that ultimate loss of innocence: the acceptance of a meaningless death.

Again and again, I decide this time I will *not* write about my illness. That's already settled, I assure myself. But again and again, I find that there is no way to change the subject. My Scheherazade fantasy involves the expectation that once I finish telling my tale I will die. A close friend asks kiddingly, "What's your next *last* book to be about?"

And so I write on. The work on my self can never be completed. Surely some day soon my storytelling will be permanently interrupted. Without realizing what I am up to, with each new book I find that I have set off on yet another path.

As an intuitive introvert, my most characteristic form of innocence is a willingness to be instructed by my dreams.

Sometimes I forget that I have a secret friend, a wise but hidden counselor, whose voice I ought to listen to more often. This counselor is my dreaming self, that part of me who sees more clearly than my waking self, whose vision is less cluttered with reason, logic, and conventional wisdom. Sometimes, when I feel stuck, even in my work, about how to deal with a situation that seems overwhelming, if I am open to listening, my dreaming self will advise me well.[9]

During the writing of *An End to Innocence*, once again it is my dreaming self that has given me direction. From the outset, without my realizing it, writing this new book has been a way of preparing for and beginning to undertake the crossing of the next threshold of personal growth. Once again, seemingly random daytime happenings have combined with mysterious night sea voyages to offer new opportunities for transformation of my ever-changing, never-changing self.

This book was conceived at a time when I believed that at last I had come to terms with not having long to live. In some measure, writing my earlier books had allowed me to accept that my death would come too soon. I had begun to understand how I might die well, with grace, and in my own way.

Then there came the series of initially bewildering dreams that first turned me toward the writing of this book. Earlier dreams and writing had prepared me for dying. How could I have guessed that this book's dreams would begin to teach me how to go on living?

These dreams began at winter's end. I was just finishing my last book [10] and entering the medically predicted period of critical tumor growth. I faced a prescheduled "routine" neurological checkup late in the spring. During this change of seasons I had been instructed to increase my vigilance for symptoms that might necessitate immediately undergoing my inevitable third (and quite possibly last) ordeal of brain surgery.

The settings for all these dreams was Martha's Vineyard Island, the family's site of summer renewal, and the place of my own annual pilgrimage to the sea.[11] In retrospect, I realize that this dream series began at a time when I was anticipating celebrating having lived through another medically uncertain year of my life. At the time my upcoming birthday coincided with the third anniversary of my last operation.

The dreams were filled with wonderfully powerful images of transformation. There were great tidal flows, surging seas, dramatically changing landscapes, and new ways to travel. Terrible storms came and went. Each time a storm had passed, the sky brightened and the water sparkled more beautifully than before the bad weather had begun. Toward the end of every dream I was sharply conscious of having survived a mighty blow. Like sea and sky, after each storm I too emerged in better shape than before the disturbance.

Each morning I could remember vividly the previous night's

dreams, but I never could understand them. This was unsettling but I felt excited. I was perplexed without feeling upset. For weeks the dreams recurred, always variations on the same themes, differing versions of the same motifs.

I felt as if my mysterious dreaming self was sending an urgent message that my reasonable everyday self simply could not decipher. In desperation, I decided to write to a West Coast psychiatrist asking his help in interpreting these dreams. This man is a madly poetic Jungian psychotherapist, a highly conscious, disturbingly intuitive human being. He is a deeply loving and beloved friend whom I have long experienced as my shadowy guide through the underground labyrinth of my unconscious. I seem to serve a parallel function for him, only my territory is the disturbingly hazy interface between his own inner and outer worlds.

Simply deciding that I would ask for help by writing to him the next morning, I discovered that the answer became available to me from within myself that very night. The final clarifying dream of the series came before I ever sat down to write the letter. The day's residue gave shape to that night's illuminating dream message. For one thing, I had been suffering through the final hours of so bad a case of the flu that I'd felt as though I were dying. Off and on all that day, I had found myself obsessing over Eliot's line about the world ending weakly with a whimper, rather than a bang. For another, whenever I'd felt well enough, I went back to reading the legend of the search for the Holy Grail. And finally, by evening I'd recovered sufficiently to wash the dishes while watching on a miniature television set an enthralling natural history documentary about that skin-shedding symbol of eternal life, the snake.

The dream series was completed that night. The resolving episode begins with my getting ready to set out on a trip to Martha's Vineyard. I have a sense of excitement and relief, as though the trip has been too long delayed. At last I'm finally about to get going, I sigh.

In this dream I am a woman. I'm having trouble getting the car packed to go. The difficulty centers on my taking along a miniature television set that I'm trying to attach to the roof. I cry out for help.

As though far away, but clearly near enough to be heard and

understood, comes another woman's voice giving me the advice I need. She tells me that to keep the T.V. in place where it belongs on top of the car, I must find the dial that brings in the educational channel frequencies and turn it as far as it will go.

Wanting to believe her, I begin turning the knob. Soon I see that there are many more numbered channels than I expected. The frequencies go up past 60! I am surprised but remain trusting of her advice.

When I have dialed as far as 60, all at once the T.V. screen lights up to reveal a bold clear caption. I understand immediately that this is the answer I have been seeking. It reads: WITHOUT DYING.

I woke up laughing. It was a lovely new morning. The first thing I did was to write to my California consultant offering my thanks for his (her) help. I told everything except what the caption said. The dream had given me a way to understand the transformation I was undergoing, I explained, but my grasp of it still felt too uncertain to be exposed.

Nonetheless I allowed my new vision to reshape my life. So far I understood that if only I would trust my feminine aspect, hope could be renewed. If I could innocently believe in powers beyond my understanding, I might yet live happily ever after (or at least a lot longer than I had expected). But whom and what to trust? The dream caption seemed to raise more questions than it answered.

I had been posed a riddle. Like some mythic hero or fairy-tale character, my life seemed to depend on my solving it correctly. Unaware at first that my writing was to be part of the search for that solution, I set out to examine the psychological implications of trust and distrust. Almost of its own accord, the book soon turned into an exploration of the loss of innocence.

Long before the answers were clear to me, they had been influencing crucial decisions. It was my immersion in the riddle posed by my dreams, and in the quest undertaken in my writing that later in the spring allowed me to refuse the recommended neurosurgery that surely would have ended my life.[12]

That fall I survived my heart attack, and for the next year went on feeling less and less defeated by the clinical fact of my being ill. The pleasures increased in living what had come to feel like an open-ended life. An added delight was my West Coast friend's establishing a monthly "transcontinental consultation practice" that included regular visits to Washington, usually with overnight stays at my house. One-and-a-half years after the riddle-posing dream series, and a few days after one of my friend's visits, I had an antic dream that summed up what I needed to know about solving the riddle. In my next letter to him I described it this way:

My major conscious purpose in writing this note is simply to express my renewed appreciation and affection for you. Having been with you again, and this time for a longer visit, had a powerful impact on me.

To make an arbitrary distinction the most obvious effects of your visit were both clinical and personal. Our having spent time together had impact on my work that reflected the sense of validation of my unconscious that I always get from you. I was able to be more immediately intuitively direct in my perception of what was going on beneath what my patients were saying, and to be bolder and more imaginative and convincing in my illuminating responses to them. Additionally, with those patients who are more open to their own unconscious (those borderline characters who are a bit crazy from time to time but frightened by their craziness, just as I sometimes am of mine), there was a marked and shared sense of ease with our craziness. The morbid aspects became more antic. The dangerous aspects seemed less deadly. Clearly we each felt less overwhelmed by the possibility of finding ourselves hopelessly lost in the morass, and so could simply enjoy these visits to the interior recesses of our imaginations.

On the personal side, for one thing, I simply had a continuing sense of well-being from having been with you, as well as a feeling that my talks with you are some of the most alive times of my life. The second piece came in the form of a dream. The synopsis of the dream could be that I found myself undergoing exploratory brain surgery in the service of some important diagnostic procedure. I was upset with the surgical aspect of it and worried about the outcome. The doctor told me not to worry, that what we had discovered was a *"white* complex something" threading its way through my brain.

When I woke from the dream, I remembered it clearly and was surprised to find that I felt just fine, both that morning and about how the dream had turned out. Two things became clear.

The first arose out of my anxious search for why I should be having a dream with that kind of medical content. It took me just a few minutes to realize that this was the anniversary of my heart attack. But then I was trying to figure out just why I was feeling so good about the dream.

As I ran it back again through my head I realized that the dream had been a joyful, comic, and an altogether delightful experience. I don't know if you know the character that Alan Alda plays in M.A.S.H. He is a super-competent, wonderfully compassionate surgeon named Hawkeye in a medical unit just behind the lines in the Korean War. He has an antic Groucho Marx-type funny/crazy ambience that saves him from becoming destructively insane. He simply will not accept the war as a sensible way to live. In the dream, Hawkeye (you) was the doctor in charge. The diagnosis that I got from him was that what was now growing inside of me was positive, increasingly conscious, and finally nourishing. It would help me to have for myself more of the antic ways in which he kept himself conscious of his inner Self throughout the war scene, maintaining his humanity no matter what he had to face.

When my oldest son was just a little kid he already understood what I am only now learning to accept: Life's riddles are posed not to be solved, but to be enjoyed. We all loved Jon's again and again asking and answering his own very favorite riddle:

Q: "What's the difference between a duck?"

A: "One of its legs is both the same!"

Obviously you will understand that there is much more to the dream. I found it a lovely set piece to celebrate both our coming together again and my having made it through another year. It begins to seem to me that I may be able to live through just about anything.

Love,
Shelly

As I complete this book I see that, for me, *there is no end to innocence.*

When I must, I face my losses squarely, accepting life as it is rather than as I would wish it to be. But from time to time, I willingly surrender to make-believe. I play at yielding to enchantment simply because pretending can make life richer and more colorful, or at least more tolerable.

There are cautions I need to observe. Should I pretend that I am *not* pretending, then I subject myself to the added needless suffering that is the price of such pseudo-innocence.

Additionally I must take care to distinguish between fantasy and politics. Like Chuang Tzu, on some dark night I may dream so vividly of fluttering gracefully in the sunlight that the next morning I may not be able to tell whether I am a man who has dreamed he was a butterfly or a butterfly who is now dreaming that he is a man. That would be a fantasy-induced problem just for me. But should I dream one night that I have given someone a gift, I must be even more careful not to expect my friend to thank me the next morning. That sort of willful confusion would create an unneeded political situation between us.

Another hazard that accompanies pretending is the anxiety that comes of trying to will that which cannot be willed. When I accept just how helpless I sometimes am, my hopelessness affords some measure of protection. False hope and the illusion of control simply make matters worse. I pay a needlessly high price whenever I forget that "only pain perceived as curable is intolerable." [13] Still, sometimes even pretending seems to work:

Consider for a moment the case of the 90-year-old man on his deathbed. (Surely the Talmud must deal with this?) Joyous and relieved over the success of his deception, for 90 years he has shielded his evil nature from public observation. For 90 years he has affected courtesy, kindness, and generosity—suppressing all the malice he knew was within him while he calculatedly and artificially substituted grace and charity. All his life he had been fooling the world into believing he was a good man. This "evil" man will, I predict, be welcomed into the kingdom of heaven. [14]

In any case, like Scheherazade, I will go on telling my own fairy tales seemingly as a way of putting off my death. But because Scheherazade really believed that her tales of the Arabian Nights could save her life, the telling of her stories became her life.

Unlike the pseudo-innocent sultana, I do what I can to avoid being bound by my own spells. Telling my tale is just my way of making the best of my life as it is. I understand that no matter what I pretend, believing my own stories will not delay my death for even a single moment. Still, it's a lovely way to pass the time.

Notes

1 : Once Upon a Time

1. Negro spiritual, "Sometimes I Feel Like a Motherless Child."
2. Joseph Campbell, "Mythological Themes in Creative Literature and Art," in *Myths, Dreams, and Religion* (New York: E. P. Dutton, 1970).
3. Marie-Louise von Franz, "The Problems of Evil in Fairy Tales," in *Evil,* ed. the Curatorium of the C. G. Jung Institute, Zurich (Evanston: Northwestern University Press, 1967), p. 85.
4. Jacob and Wilhelm Grimm, "The Three Feathers." Quoted in Marie-Louise von Franz, *An Introduction to the Interpretation of Fairy Tales* (New York: Spring Publications, 1970), pp. 1–3.
5. Bruno Bettelheim, *The Uses of Enchantment: The Meaning and Importance of Fairy Tales* (New York: Alfred A. Knopf, 1976), p. 8; italics added.
6. See Rollo May, *Power and Innocence: A Search for the Source of Violence* (New York: Dell Publishing Co., Delta Book, 1972), pp. 49ff.
7. Rollo May, *The Courage to Create* (New York: W. W. Norton, 1975), pp. 52–55.
8. Ibid., p. 53; italics added.

4 : The Magic Helper

1. Eugene Delacroix. Quoted on book jacket of *The Great Mother and Other Poems* by Michele Murray (New York: Sheed and Ward, 1974).
2. Leslie Farber, "Perfectibility and the Psychoanalytic Candidate," in *The Ways of the Will: Essays Toward a Psychopathology of the Will* (New York: Basic Books, 1966), p. 219.
3. See E. Fuller Torrey, *The Mind Game: Witchdoctors and Psychiatrists* (New York: Bantam Books, 1972), pp. 15–33.
4. This term was first used by Carl Whitaker (private correspondence).

5   :   *If You Want to Know the Truth . . .*

1. J. D. Salinger, *The Catcher in the Rye* (Boston: Little, Brown, 1945).

2. Ibid., pp. 224–25.

3. Jean Piaget and Barbel Inhelder, *The Origin of Chance in Children,* trans. Lowell Leake, Jr., Paul Burrell, and Harold D. Fishbein (New York: W. W. Norton, 1975). The children were asked to account for the random results of tossing batches of counters. Each coinlike counter had a cross on one side and a circle on the other. Before each toss the children were asked to pick how many would land heads and how many tails. After the toss, each was asked to explain the distribution.

4. Url Lanham, *The Insects* (New York: Columbia University Press, 1964), pp. 44–45; italics added.

5. Sheldon B. Kopp, et al., *The Naked Therapist: A Collection of Embarrassments* (San Diego: EdITS, 1976), p. 17.

6. Albert Camus, *The Myth of Sisyphus and Other Essays,* trans. Justin O'Brien (New York: Vintage Books, 1959), p. 5.

6   :   *Momma's Boy and Daddy's Little Girl*

1. Gustave Flaubert, *Madame Bovary: A Story of Provincial Life,* trans. Alan Russell (Baltimore: Penguin Books, 1950).

2. Martin Turnell, "Madame Bovary," in *Flaubert, A Collection of Critical Essays,* ed. Raymond Giraud (Englewood Cliffs: Prentice-Hall, 1964), p. 100.

3. Even the total ruin with which this simple tragedy ended was not harsh enough to satisfy the societal hypocrisy of nineteenth-century France. Following the publication of *Madame Bovary* in the *Revue de Paris,* Flaubert was tried for offending public morals.

4. Flaubert, *Madame Bovary,* pp. 54, 56–57.

5. Ibid., p. 175.

6. Ibid., p. 49.

7. Ibid., p. 98.

8. Leslie Tonner, *Nothing But the Best: The Luck of the Jewish Princess* (New York: Coward, McCann & Geoghegan, 1975). Though this defense of the position centers mainly on daughters, it is a colorful description of some of the child-raising emphases in Jewish-American families.

7 : Pollyanna and the Paranoid

1. When I write of the pseudo-innocent paranoid neurotic character style, I do not mean to include the more catastrophic state of delusional madness. Psychotic paranoia is a terrifying experience. I've been through it and I don't recommend it. Simply feeling singled out for attack would be frightening enough. Frantically trying to protect yourself from enemies when you can't distinguish between what's real and what's unreal creates an overwhelming experience of helpless vulnerability. In desperation you must summon up every bit of self-protective cunning, only to discover that the forces of evil cannot be overcome.

2. Sheldon B. Kopp, *If You Meet the Buddha on the Road, Kill Him!: The Pilgrimage of Psychotherapy Patients* (Palo Alto: Science and Behavior Books, 1972), pp. 212–13.

3. Voltaire, *Candide,* trans. John Butt (Baltimore: Penguin Books, 1947).

4. Thomas A. Harris, *I'm O.K.—You're O.K.* (New York: Harper & Row, 1967).

5. William Sloane Coffin, Jr. Quip quoted in *The New York Times,* August 11, 1977, p. 16.

8 : Too Good to Be True

1. See chapt. 3, "The Heroic Adventurer."

2. There were a few exceptions who were quite unlike the young, sweet murderers I had known at the reformatory. Mostly they tended to be armed robbers, characteristically brutal men who had killed someone in the course of one of their habitual assaults.

3. Herman Melville, "Billy Budd, Sailor (an inside narrative)," in *Billy Budd, Sailor and Other Stories,* selected and edited by Harold Beaver (Baltimore: Penguin Books, 1967), pp. 317–409.

4. F. P. Matthiessen, "Billy Budd, Foretopman," in *Melville, A Collection of Critical Essays,* ed. Richard Chase (Englewood Cliffs: Prentice-Hall, 1962), p. 157.

5. Melville, "Billy Budd," p. 360.

6. Ibid., p. 376.

7. Ibid., p. 378.

8. Ibid., p. 400.

9. Dietrich Bonhoeffer, *Letters and Papers from Prison,* rev. edn., ed. Eberhard Bethge (New York: Macmillan, 1972), pp. 7f.

10. When complaints such as these come from a female patient, the sexist political problems must be sorted out from the neurotic ones. This sort of depression in a compliant woman trapped in a traditional marriage will have large components of non-neurotic unhappiness constituting a realistic response to an oppressive life situation. To this aspect of the depression, the therapist can be helpful only by offering a clarifying and supportive, explicitly feminist posture, one that validates the sanity of the patient's feeling upset.

9 : *Someone to Look After Me*

1. John Steinbeck, *Of Mice and Men* (New York: Viking Press, 1937).
2. Ibid., p. 44.
3. Ibid., pp. 14–16.
4. Virginia Woolf, *Orlando: A Biography,* with an Afterword by Elizabeth Bowen (New York: New American Library, Signet Classic, 1960), p. 43 (originally published in 1928).
5. Ivan Illich, *Medical Nemesis: The Expropriation of Health* (New York: Pantheon Books, 1976).
6. Sheldon B. Kopp, *Guru: Metaphors from a Psychotherapist* (Palo Alto: Science and Behavior Books, 1971), p. 162.

10 : *Communal Innocence*

1. Rollo May, *Power and Innocence: A Search for the Sources of Violence* (New York: Dell Publishing, Delta Book, 1972), p. 21.
2. Northrop Frye, *The Secular Scripture: A Study of the Structure of Romance* (Cambridge, Mass.: Harvard University Press, 1976), p. 4.
3. Joseph Campbell, *The Masks of God,* vol. I–IV (New York: Viking Press, 1962).
4. Joseph Campbell, "Mythological Themes in Creative Literature and Art," in *Myths, Dreams, and Religion,* ed. Joseph Campbell (New York: E. P. Dutton paperback, 1970), pp. 138–75.
5. Ibid., p. 138.
6. Sheldon B. Kopp, *The Hanged Man: Psychotherapy and the Forces of Darkness* (Palo Alto: Science and Behavior Books, 1974), p. 12.
7. Plato, *The Republic: Book VII,* in *Dialogs of Plato,* vol. I, trans. B. Jowett (New York: Random House, 1937), pp. 515ff.
8. H. G. Wells, "The Country of the Blind," in *The Complete Short Stories of H. G. Wells* (London: Ernest Benn, 1927), pp. 167–92.
9. Ibid., p. 180.
10. Ibid.

11. Ibid., p. 179.

12. Ibid., p. 188.

13. William Kilpatrick, *Identity and Intimacy* (New York: Dell Publishing Co., Delta Book, 1975), pp. 66–67.

14. Sheldon B. Kopp, "Person Envy," *Journal of Contemporary Psychotherapy* 6, no. 2 (Summer 1974): 154–56. In slightly different form, this vignette first appeared as a journal article.

15. Arthur Koestler, Richard Wright, Louis Fischer, Ignazio Silone, André Gide, Stephen Spender, *The God That Failed,* ed. Richard Crossman (New York: Bantam Books, 1951).

16. Sheldon B. Kopp, *Guru: Metaphors from a Psychotherapist* (Palo Alto: Science and Behavior Books, 1971), p. 41.

17. Lewis Carroll, *Alice's Adventures in Wonderland and Through the Looking-Glass,* with all the original illustrations by Sir John Tenniel (New York: St. Martin's Press, 1968).

18. Donald Rackin, "Alice's Journey to the End of the Night," *PMLA,* 81 (1966), 313–26.

19. Ibid., p. 412.

20. Ibid., p. 414.

21. Ibid., p. 415.

11 : Making the Best of It

1. Ernest Becker, *Escape from Evil* (New York: Free Press, 1975), p. 33; italics added.

2. Ernest Becker, *The Denial of Death* (New York: Free Press, 1973), p. 60.

3. See Paul Tillich, *The Courage to Be* (New Haven: Yale University Press, 1952), pp. 40–55.

4. Johan Huizinga, *Homo Ludens: A Study of the Play Element in Culture* (Boston: Beacon Press, 1950), p. 11.

5. Ibid., p. 10.

6. Northrop Frye, *The Secular Scripture: A Study of the Structure of Romance* (Cambridge, Mass.: Harvard University Press, 1976), p. 166.

7. See chapt. 9, "Someone to Look After Me," pp. 113–36.

8. Sheldon B. Kopp, *Guru: Metaphors from a Psychotherapist* (1971), pp. 159–66 and *If You Meet the Buddha on the Road, Kill Him!: The Pilgrimage of Psychotherapy Patients* (1972), pp. 157–59. Both published by Science and Behavior Books, Palo Alto.

9. Sheldon B. Kopp, *The Hanged Man: Psychotherapy and the Forces of Darkness* (Palo Alto: Science and Behavior Books, 1974), p. 205.

10. Sheldon B. Kopp, et al., *The Naked Therapist: A Collection of Embarrassments* (San Diego: EdITS Publishers, 1976).

11. Sheldon B. Kopp, *If You Meet the Buddha on the Road* . . . , pp. 153-59.

12. See chapt. 9, "Someone to Look After Me," pp. 113-36.

13. Ivan Illich, *Medical Nemesis: The Expropriation of Health* (New York: Pantheon Books, 1976), p. 134.

14. Willard Gaylin, "What You See Is the Real You," op-ed page of *The New York Times,* October 7, 1977.